From Trauma to Trial

Copyright © 2020 by William J. Teggart

All rights reserved. No part of this book may be reproduced or transmitted in any form or by any means without written permission from the author.

Printed in the USA.

From
TRAUMA
to
TRIAL

*A Step-by-Step Guide
to Ontario Personal Injury Law*

WILLIAM J. TEGGART B.A., LL.B.

DEDICATION

To Nancy, who took a chance on a law student she met at a charity bowling tournament. Thank you for always loving and believing in me.

To Reighan and Sydney, being your Dad is the single most rewarding role I have in life. I'm so proud of the strong, independent young women you have become.

To Mom, for the unwavering love that only a mother can give.

And to Dad, you were my greatest mentor and inspired me to become a lawyer. You taught me to become a student of my profession. This book is an effort to pay it forward to those in need. I know one day we'll meet again. NGU.

Work Hard ~ Be Honest ~ Be Fair ~ Stand Your Ground
Moses Teggart

Acknowledgements

This book would not have been possible without the contributions and support of many who have helped me throughout the years.

I would never have succeeded in the practice of law without the lessons instilled by my college hockey coach, Gary Wright. As the head coach of the American International College Yellow Jackets, he taught us that hard work, focus and discipline wins championships — a lesson that carries over into life, and the practice of law.

I want to acknowledge my legal mentor of many years, Roger Oatley. I wouldn't be the lawyer I am today without his support and guidance. When you work with a legal giant like Roger for so long, you absorb countless lessons. There is no question that some of these lessons made their way onto the pages of this book.

In addition, I would like to acknowledge my team at Teggart Injury Law: Sharon Geniole, Leanne Clarkson, Vanessa Locicero, and Nancy Teggart. I could not do what I do without their expertise and professionalism. Each of them carries a profound sense of empathy for our clients who are facing tremendous challenges. They understand that these people should not have to feel as if they were having a wisdom tooth pulled when attending our offices. They inject a positivity to our firm that benefits our clients, many of whom are struggling through the worst days of their lives.

This book would not have been possible without the inspiration of my good friend, former client, and Team Canada sledge hockey Paralympian, Kevin Rempel. I recommend Kevin's book, *Still Standing*, to anyone living through a traumatic event. Kevin's friendship, support, and inspiration throughout this process have been invaluable.

My good friend, Craig Markou, has offered his expertise and experience as a creative director for a very long time. I appreciate all of the work he has done and the support he has provided over the years, including his assistance with this book.

My law school classmate, Brad White, of Osler, Hoskin & Harcourt, is one of Canada's top intellectual property litigators. Brad earns more international Air Miles than anyone I know, and I have very much appreciated his time, support, and encouragement.

My colleague, and one of Ontario's foremost personal injury lawyers, Mike Smitiuch, of Smitiuch Injury Law, was a great source of support for me in this process. He gave freely of his time to review sections of the book and I am grateful for his insights.

My editor, Julie Winn was both an inspiration and a blessing. She brought a keen intellect and clarity of thought to the editorial process. In short, she was a true partner for me. I recommend Julie to anyone looking for a talented editor. She can be reached through WINNcreative.ca.

Finally, I want to thank all of my past and current clients for the trust they have placed in me. Hiring a personal injury lawyer is in some ways like inviting a stranger into your home. These people have welcomed me into their lives and made me feel like part of their families. They inspire me to be a better lawyer and they each serve as a testament to the resilience of the human spirit.

Contents

ACKNOWLEDGEMENTS vii

PREFACE xix

INTRODUCTION xxi

   1. The Case of Marilyn and Her Son Joe xxi
   2. Levelling the Economic Playing Field xxiv
   3. An Uphill Battle xxv
   4. Light at the End of the Tunnel xxvi
   5. What to Expect From This Book and Who Can
      Benefit From Reading It xxviii

Chapter 1. What to Do in the Days Following a Serious Personal Injury 1

   1. Gather All Insurance Documents 2
   2. Take Notes or Make a Diary for Future Litigation 4
   3. Take Photographs of Injuries 4
   4. Take Photographs of the Scene or Any Property Damage 5
   5. Keep All Receipts and Mileage Records 6
   6. Defer Speaking to an Insurance Adjuster Until After
      You Have Hired a Lawyer 6

   Teggart's Bottom Line 8

Chapter 2. **Why Hire a Lawyer Early?** 9
1. Don't Miss Important Notice Periods 9
2. Don't Miss an Important Limitation Period 10
3. The Investigation Should Begin Immediately..11
4. The Insurance Company Will Be Investigating Early...............................12
5. Waiting Delays Your Case and Makes You More Vulnerable
During Settlement Negotiations 13

Teggart's Bottom Line 15

Chapter 3. **Common Obstacles to Finding the Right Lawyer** 17
1. "I Don't Know If I Need a Lawyer" 18
2. "I'm Not the Suing Type" 18
3. The Reputation of Personal Injury Lawyers..19
4. "I Can't Afford a Lawyer" 20
5. "I Don't Want to Sue a Loved One Who Was at Fault for a Car Crash" 21

Teggart's Bottom Line 23

Chapter 4. **How to Find the Right Personal Injury Lawyer** 25
1. Training of Personal Injury Lawyers...26
2. Personal Injury Law Firms 101 27
3. How to Find a Personal Injury Lawyer..28
   A. Google Searching..28
   B. Word of Mouth 28
4. How to Research Qualifications Online..29
   A. Areas of Practice 29
   B. Former Client Reviews and Testimonials 30
   C. Social Media Accounts, Blog Posts, and Videos..................................31
5. Red Flags...32
   A. Solicitation Calls and Visits..32
   B. Awards 32
   C. Previous Judgments and Settlements 33
   D. Other Patients in Hospitals 34

Teggart's Bottom Line 35

Chapter 5. **The First Meeting With a Personal Injury Lawyer 37**
    1. What Do I Need to Have With Me at the First Meeting?......................37
    2. How Long Will the Meeting Last?..38
    3. Solicitor-Client Confidentiality 39
    4. What Issues Will the Lawyer Cover in the Meeting?.........................39
    5. The Contingency Fee Retainer Agreement..40
        A. *General Information*..*40*
        B. *How a Typical Contingency Fee Retainer Agreement Works*.......*43*
        C. *Typical Percentages Lawyers Charge in Contingency*
            Fee Retainer Agreements..*44*
        D. *The Contingency Fee Retainer Agreement: A Cautionary Note*.................*45*
    6. What Won't Be Covered in Your First Meeting?..................................45
    7. How Do I Decide Whether to Hire the Lawyer?.................................46
    8. What If I Want to Fire My Personal Injury Lawyer?..........................48
    Teggart's Bottom Line 50

Chapter 6. **Dangers of Social Media Accounts, Surveillance, and the Importance of Confidentiality 51**
    1. Dangers of Social Media Use 51
    2. Dangers of Insurance Company Surveillance......................................53
    3. Risks of Discussing Your Case with Healthcare Providers 54
    Teggart's Bottom Line 56

Chapter 7. **Personal Injury Law 101 – What You Need to Know.....57**
    1. Liability..58
        A. *Who Is at Fault?*..*58*
        B. *Contributory Negligence: Was the Injured Person Also at Fault?*.............*59*
        C. *What If More Than One Party Is at Fault?*....................................*60*
    2. Damages: The Value of Your Case..60
        A. *Loss of Income/Earning Capacity and Pension Losses*................*61*
        B. *Care Costs*..*62*
        C. *Housekeeping and Maintenance Expenses* *63*
        D. *General Damages for Pain and Suffering* *64*

    E. Out-of-Pocket Expenses 65
    F. Family Law Act Claims 66
    G. Punitive Damages 67
  3. Causation: Did the Person Cause Your Injury? 67
    A. Causation: General Information 67
    B. Thin Skull and Crumbling Skull Cases 68
  4. The Standard of Proof 70
    A. General Information 70
    B. Future Losses 70
  Teggart's Bottom Line 72

Chapter 8. **Starting a Lawsuit** 75
  1. The Statement of Claim 75
    A. The Parties: Who is Suing Whom? 76
    B. The Prayer for Relief: How Much Is Being Claimed? 76
    C. Who Are the Parties and Where Do They Reside? 77
    D. What Happened? 77
    E. Allegations of Negligence 77
    F. Injuries and Impairments 78
    G. Claims for Damages 78
    H. Legislation and Place of Trial 79
  2. Jury Notice or Not? 79
  3. Will My Case Go to Trial If I Sue Someone? 80
  4. What Happens If I Change My Mind and Decide Not to Sue? 80
  5. What Happens After the Lawsuit Is Started? 81
  Teggart's Bottom Line 82

Chapter 9. **Examinations for Discovery** 85
  1. What Are Examinations for Discovery? 85
  2. Where Do Examinations for Discovery Take Place? 86
  3. What Do I Wear to My Examination for Discovery? 87
  4. Typical Areas of Questioning by the Defence Lawyer 87

CONTENTS xv

    5. Preparation for Your Examination for Discovery 88
    6. How Do Examinations for Discovery Work? 90
    7. Do Examinations for Discovery Have Rules? 91
    8. How Long Will My Examination for Discovery Last? 92
    Teggart's Bottom Line 93

Chapter 10. **Post-Examinations for Discovery Events** 95
    1. Medical-Legal Examinations and Other Expert Reports 95
        A. Your Medical-Legal Examinations..*95*
        B. Medical-Legal Examinations Required by the Defence *97*
        C. Other Expert Opinions *98*
    2. Fulfilling Undertakings and Motions 98
    3. Focus Groups 99
    Teggart's Bottom Line 101

Chapter 11. **Mediation** 103
    1. What Is a Mediation? 103
    2. The Players: Who Attends a Mediation and What Are Their Roles? 104
        A. The Mediator... *104*
        B. The Injured Person, Their Lawyer, and Family Members........................ *104*
        C. The Insurance Defence Lawyer and the Insurance
           Company Representative *105*
        D. Others.. *106*
    3. Before the Mediation, and Your Mindset Going into it 107
        A. Mediation Briefs... *107*
        B. Meeting With Your Lawyer Before the Mediation *108*
        C. Expectations and Mindset *108*
    4. How Does a Mediation Work?.. 109
        A. The Venue.. *109*
        B. Preliminary Remarks by the Mediator *110*
        C. Your Lawyer's Opening Statement *110*
        D. The Defence Lawyer's Opening Statement.. *111*

  E. Caucusing and Negotiations 112

  F. Settlement 113

 5. What Happens If My Case Doesn't Settle at a Mediation? 114

 Teggart's Bottom Line 116

Chapter 12. **Pre-Trial Conferences** **117**

 1. What Is a Pre-Trial Conference? 117

 2. How Does the Pre-Trial Conference Work? 118

 Teggart's Bottom Line 121

Chapter 13. **Trial** **123**

 1. How Long Does a Trial Last? 123

 2. Jury or No Jury? 124

 3. Choosing the Jury 125

 4. Pre-Trial Motions and Preliminary Issues 127

 5. Opening Addresses 128

 6. Simplified Rules Cases 129

 7. The Plaintiff's Case 129

  A. The Witnesses 130

   (i) Lay Witnesses 130

   (ii) Expert Witnesses 130

   (iii) Treating Medical Experts 131

  B. Direct Examinations and Cross-Examinations 131

  C. How the Questioning Works 132

  D. Completion of the Plaintiff's Case 133

 8. The Case for the Defendant/Insurance Company 133

 9. Mid-Trial Conferences 134

 10. Reply Evidence 134

 11. Closing Statements 135

 12. Charge to the Jury 136

 13. Jury Deliberations and Verdict 136

 Teggart's Bottom Line 138

Chapter 14. **Life After a Lawsuit** 141
    1. Is It Really Over? The Right to Appeal 141
    2. How Does It Feel to Have the Case Behind You? 142
    3. Taxation of Money from Settlement or Verdict 143
    4. Structured Settlements, Investments, and Finances 144
    5. Don't Discuss the Settlement or Verdict Amount 145
    6. Have a Will and Power of Attorney Prepared or Reviewed 146
    Teggart's Bottom Line 147

GLOSSARY OF PERSONAL INJURY LAW TERMS 149
APPENDIX A: ACCIDENT BENEFITS SUMMARY CHART 153
APPENDIX B: EXAMPLE STATEMENT OF CLAIM 154

Preface

Over the last 22 years, I have met thousands of new clients and there is one thought that so many of them share with me: "I've never been through this before." These people are experiencing a roller coaster of emotions as a result of their injuries or the injury—or even death—of a loved one. They may be in shock, they may be grieving, and they may be feeling hopeless.

Often, friends and family members have recommended that they call a personal injury lawyer, but they have been hesitant. They cling to the hope that things will return to normal, but they also know that the unfortunate reality is that they may not. They are wary of personal injury lawyers, given the negative reputation this profession has, and the questionable advertisements they see on television. At the same time, they've heard horror stories about dealing with insurance companies and they know they really need some help.

In addition, they know very little about the law or how lawsuits work and are fearful about potential legal costs. Almost everything they believe about personal injury law comes from the media.

This book is for you if you find yourself in these unfortunate circumstances.

By writing this book, my goal has been to shed some light on the legal system and provide you with a sense of what to expect after a serious personal injury. Information is power, and my hope is that by providing this information, I can help reduce your anxiety so that you can make it through the next step. Recovery—from physical, psychological, and even legal perspectives—is a step-by-step process. You need to take it one day at a time.

I do not intend this book to serve as a self-representation guide; however, I do strongly encourage you to consult with an experienced personal injury lawyer if you or a family member has suffered a serious personal injury or death. Personal injury law in Ontario is complex and every case is different. My hope is that the information in this guide will help you to better understand the legal process you may be going through.

If you are beginning this journey, I wish you the best of luck with your case! Should you have any questions, I invite you to visit **www.teggartinjurylaw.com** or e-mail me directly at **bill@teggartinjurylaw.com**.

Bill Teggart, B.A., LL.B.
William J. Teggart Personal Injury Law P.C.
Barrie, Ontario
December 2019

INTRODUCTION

I became a personal injury lawyer because I am hard-wired to help people. As a personal injury lawyer, I guide injured people and their families through the legal system—often during the worst days of their lives. Despite the negative stigma surrounding personal injury lawyers, I firmly believe that mine is an honourable calling.

I see incredible tragedy and suffering on a regular basis. My clients need legal help, and I am honoured that they trust me and my team to provide it to them.

Most of my clients and their families experience emotional turmoil as they attempt to come to terms with their losses, while navigating our complex medical, legal, and insurance systems. What follows is a hypothetical scenario that may resonate with you. The legal system is far from perfect, but you'll learn that there is light at the end of the tunnel.

1. The Case of Marilyn and Her Son Joe

Marilyn is on the night shift when she gets the call. It sends her into a spiral. A police officer explains that her 19-year-old son Joe has been seriously hurt in a car crash. Paramedics have taken him to a local hospital by ambulance. His injuries are so severe, however, that the hospital has arranged for Ornge helicopter transportation to a trauma hospital in Toronto, where they can better handle his medical care.

Marilyn hangs up the phone, grabs her purse, and runs to her car. She drives home, throws a few items into her overnight bag, and heads for the city, making her way straight to the Toronto hospital in tears. The situation doesn't sound good, and she fears that Joe may not make it. She does her best to keep a positive attitude, but in the back of her mind she's thinking "parents aren't supposed to lose their children."

After finding a spot in the crowded hospital parking lot, Marilyn jumps out, runs in, and makes her way to the information desk. The area is like a beehive, with people hustling in every direction. After getting hurried instructions on where to find the Neurological Intensive Care Unit (NICU), she walks around in circles, trying to find the right elevator. Frustrated, she returns to the information desk and thankfully, a hospital volunteer is able to guide her to the elevator and up to the nursing station of the NICU.

As Marilyn walks down the halls, she hears the constant beeping and insistent alarms of medical devices. She peers into each small room, looking for her son, but all she sees are nurses, and patients in varying states of consciousness, attached to many machines.

Nurses direct her to Joe's room. She walks in and is hit by the smell of medication and urine. She finds Joe unconscious, attached to tubes, bags, and drips that are helping to keep him alive. His head is bandaged and his eyes are swollen shut. There is a tube down his throat which she assumes is helping him breathe. No one has bothered to clean the blood off his face. Doctors and nurses are understandably more concerned with keeping him alive.

INTRODUCTION

After asking around for what seems like forever, Marilyn finally meets the doctor who has assessed and treated Joe. The doctor explains that Joe has suffered a severe brain injury in the crash. His brain is bleeding. They have implanted something called an *intracranial pressure monitor*. If the pressure within Joe's skull becomes too high, they will have to perform life-saving surgery called a craniotomy.

Over the hours and days that follow, Marilyn spends most of her days at Joe's bedside. She lives minute by minute in survival mode. Initially, other family members visit on a regular basis. There are good days and bad days, and a lot of waiting. She wonders daily whether she will hear from the doctor, how Joe is really doing, and whether or not he is in the clear. The visits from friends and family taper off over time. Marilyn often sits alone all day long beside Joe's bed in a hospital chair that looks like a remnant from World War II and is about as comfortable as you might imagine such a relic to be.

She just wants her son back. Eventually, he regains consciousness, and begins to breathe on his own. Initially, Joe has no idea where he is or who Marilyn is. He has no idea what happened to him. He can barely speak and when he does, his speech is garbled, and he makes little sense.

The police contact Marilyn. The officer explains that Joe was hit by a drunk driver. The breath sample showed that the drunk driver had over twice the legal limit of alcohol in his system. It was his first offence though. If he is convicted—which is not a given—he will probably spend no time in jail. He will likely lose his driver's license for one year.

Joe continues a long and painful recovery, but doctors tell him and his mother that he will never return to normal. They remain optimistic, but there is a chance Joe may never be able to work. He faces a lifetime of rehabilitation. Marilyn thinks to herself, "...*and the drunk driver just gets a license suspension and a fine. How are we supposed to pay for all of this care? How is Joe going to live and pay his rent when he can't work?*"

This roller coaster of emotions that Marilyn experiences continues for many years. There are good days and awful days. While Joe has survived, Marilyn knows that he will never have the life he was supposed to have had. And her role has now shifted from Mom to nurse, caregiver, and social worker, depending on the day.

2. Levelling the Economic Playing Field

Stories like this play out every day. Through little or no fault of their own, injured people and their families suffer the painful consequences of the disastrous choices made by others: a drunk driver; the truck driver who runs a red light; the boat operator who fails to use their navigational lights; the property owner who fails to safely maintain their property.

Our system of criminal law is designed to punish the offender and deter others. But the victims are left to pick up the pieces themselves.

Often, victims need help because the financial consequences they face are insurmountable. Government-funded programs are overburdened. You never seem to get to the front of the line waiting for government-funded services. Income continuation insurance benefits are accessible; however, they are usually not enough to allow you to make ends meet.

At this point, the *civil* justice system can come into play. Understanding how it works and taking appropriate action can lead to victims' receiving payment for the losses they (or their family members) have suffered. We have all heard the saying "Money doesn't buy happiness." While this may be true, money from a personal injury lawsuit does help people with no means to pay their mortgage, put food on the table, and assist with the much-needed care they require. In short, a personal injury lawsuit helps level the economic playing field that was thrown out of balance by the poor decisions of another.

3. An Uphill Battle

Because most people have no experience with the legal system, they do not realize that recovering money for their losses will be an uphill battle. In time, they realize that they have to contend with not only a lengthy and painful rehabilitation process, but also an insurance company that will do its best to stand in their way.

The vast majority of personal injury claims are covered by insurance. That is, at-fault parties will have insurance to protect themselves if they are sued. The insurance company will pay for a lawyer to defend them in a personal injury lawsuit. The insurer will also pay for any settlement or amount determined by a verdict, up to the limits of the insurance policy. But as bizarre as it may sound, our court rules prevent the jury that is deciding a case from even knowing whether or not a defendant *has* insurance. There is no question that some jury verdicts are skewed against the injured person because the jurors believe that the at-fault person will be paying the judgment out of personal savings.

Insurance companies have significant financial resources they can use to defend injury claims, and frankly, it is in their best interests to do just this. Avoiding payment helps their bottom line, so they work hard to win their cases.

In many ways, our legal system favours these insurers. There are caps on the amount of money a court can award in a personal injury case. The Supreme Court of Canada capped the maximum amount a person can receive for pain and suffering and loss of enjoyment of life. There are similar limits on how much a court can award to family members of an injured or deceased person. In car crash cases and boating accident cases, there are several legal rules which can serve to reduce or even eliminate an injured person's claims.

I've represented injured people and their families for over 22 years and can say with certainty that these challenges weigh heavily on many of them. As they struggle to rehabilitate from their injuries, they also face an insurance company's scrutiny in their fight for justice. They feel as though every aspect of their life is under a microscope and this adds to the stress and anxiety they are experiencing.

The bottom line is that this is an adversarial process. You and your personal injury lawyer will have to fight for what's fair.

4. Light at the End of the Tunnel

I've given many million-dollar and multi-million-dollar cheques to seriously injured people and their family members at the conclusion of their lawsuits. Unlike what many would believe, however, these folks are rarely happy. At best, they are relieved. Relieved that their lawsuit is over, and relieved that they will have money to survive and pay for their care. In these final meetings, I see far more tears than smiles.

I keep in touch with many of my former clients after their cases resolve, however, and I can say there is light at the end of the tunnel. While money for their losses cannot magically return their health and well-being, many of them manage to live productive and happy lives.

Many of my former clients inspire me. Paul Plewa, for example, suffered a spinal cord injury in a motocross crash. He has recently started his own wellness company, and he gave an inspirational speech at TEDx McMaster U in December 2019. I have former clients with brain injuries who now relish their roles as a new mom or dad. My former client and good friend Kevin Rempel suffered a spinal cord injury and became a Paralympian. He earned a bronze medal for the Team Canada sledge hockey team in the Sochi Paralympics. Kevin is an inspirational speaker and operates the Sledge Hockey Experience, which gives corporations the opportunity to learn about inclusion and team building (www.playsledgehockey.com). His book, *Still Standing – When You Have Every Reason to Give Up, Keep Going*, is recommended reading for anyone recovering from spinal cord injury or other major trauma.[1]

Just as important, I have clients with the peace of mind of knowing that they have the financial resources to provide for themselves and their families. The point is that the process is difficult but with strong guidance, you will get through it.

---

[1] Kevin's book is available at kevinrempel.com.

5. What to Expect From This Book and Who Can Benefit From Reading It

This book tells you what experienced personal injury lawyers and insurance defence lawyers know about personal injury law. Although reading it is not a substitute for engaging the services of an expert, the book is designed as a guide to help you learn what to expect from the legal system after a serious personal injury or the accident-related death of a family member.

This book covers what happens from the time of the initial injury or death, to the point at which you find a personal injury lawyer. It then takes you through the various stages in the legal process, up to and including a trial. This is meant to guide an injured person, their family, and rehabilitation providers in a chronological way through the entire litigation process. Here is a snapshot of what you will learn about:

- important things you or your family members should do immediately following a serious injury in order to protect your rights;
- why you should hire a lawyer soon after a serious personal injury;
- how to overcome obstacles to finding and retaining the right lawyer for you or your family member;
- what to expect in the first meeting with a personal injury lawyer;
- the dangers of surveillance and social media usage following injury;
- how lawyers and courts determine the value of a personal injury case, including how issues of fault are decided;
- what a personal injury lawsuit is and how it begins;
- all about a process called *examinations for discovery*, including important facts you should know before attending;

- what a mediation is and what to expect in the process;
- what a pre-trial conference is and what to expect at this meeting;
- all about the workings of a personal injury trial; and
- what life is like after a personal injury lawsuit resolves.

At the end of each chapter, you will find a section called, "Teggart's Bottom Line." These sections are meant to be a simple summary of the important aspects of each chapter.

At the conclusion of the book, I've included a glossary of legal terms that are often used in personal injury law. This is meant as an easy reference to help familiarize you with the many complicated terms used in a personal injury lawsuit.

The Government of Ontario has recently changed some laws that will affect more modest personal injury claims. Specifically, it has increased the jurisdiction of Small Claims Court from $25,000 to $35,000—meaning Small Claims Court now handles cases in this value range. Likewise, it has increased the threshold of *Simplified Procedure* cases from $100,000 to $200,000. Cases brought under these new rules will follow different procedures than the larger cases on which I focus in this book. Since the new rules only came into force in January 2020, it is not yet clear exactly how they will affect personal injury cases. To the extent to which I felt it might be helpful however, I have referenced the new procedures throughout.

Who can benefit from this book? In short, people who are suffering the consequences of someone else's mistake or intentional act, including:
- seriously injured people;
- the friends and families of seriously injured people;

- the family of a person who died as a result of injuries they suffered;
- healthcare providers trying to understand the legal system and how it impacts their patients and clients; and
- young paralegals and lawyers beginning their careers in the field of personal injury law.

It is important to point out that each and every personal injury case is different. This means that some of what you'll read in the book may not apply to your specific case. Moreover, the advice I provide in this book is the general advice I give all my clients. In each of their cases however, I also give them advice specific to their claims. Whatever the nature of your case, I encourage you to speak with an experienced personal injury lawyer.

Unfortunately, this is a complex area of law—and one that does not lend itself to self-representation by an injured person. This book, therefore, is not meant to be a self-representation guide; rather, a guide to help you understand what to expect in the process of a personal injury lawsuit.

It is my hope that by reading this book you will feel you are better informed about this process. By learning about it, you will reduce the anxiety that comes with the unknown. I understand that you've never been through this before, and I hope you find this material helpful along the way.

CHAPTER ONE

What to Do in the Days Following a Serious Personal Injury

Family and friends are often on hand at the hospital following a serious injury to a loved one. They may spend long hours feeling stressed out in cramped patient rooms and waiting rooms.

Communications with hospital staff are often frustrating. New doctors and nurses are constantly rotating in and out. Sometimes these people provide helpful information and other times…not so much. Unfortunately, this can leave an injured person and their family feeling rather helpless.

Positive action can be taken, however, during the hours and days that follow an injury. In fact, there are important things that injured people (if they are able) or family members of an injured person can do to protect their interests in this difficult and unfamiliar situation. This chapter is about all of these things.

1. Gather all Insurance Documents

Despite a person's being seriously injured, their bills continue to roll in. The bank still expects the mortgage payment, and someone still needs to take care of car payments, household bills, and other monthly expenses.

Just as important, an injured person may require expensive community-based rehabilitation following hospital discharge. Someone may have to pay for this rehabilitation and it's important to understand whether or not insurance benefits are available.

Following an injury, it's helpful to look for insurance documents that describe any benefits that you may be entitled to following a serious injury. It's important to review all of the insurance documents so you can get the ball rolling on the application process for any benefits that you may be entitled to. Depending on your coverage, you may need to review the following:

Extended healthcare coverage booklets from an employer

These are usually available through the human resources department. They describe the benefits a person may be entitled to and clarify whether or not the costs of physiotherapy, psychological counselling, occupational therapy, or items like assistive devices may be covered;

Short-term disability and long-term disability benefits booklets from an employer

Short-term disability benefits are usually payable after a limited period following an injury—typically 120 days or less—if the person cannot return to work. These benefits, as their name suggests, do not last for long. If the injured person cannot return to work for an extended period of time, long-term disability benefits may be available. Typically, short-term disability benefits pay between 70 and 100 percent of an injured person's salary, while long-term disability benefits usually pay approximately 66 percent of a person's pre-injury salary. The employer should be able to provide details of any available disability benefits.

Critical injury insurance

These benefits are sometimes included in an employee's benefits package—particularly with unionized employees—or may sometimes be purchased privately. They usually provide lump-sum payments if the person has suffered certain specific injuries or impairments.

Mortgage insurance

Some people purchase mortgage insurance, which covers their mortgage payments if they become injured and cannot work. A contact at the bank holding the mortgage should be able to provide this information.

A life insurance policy

Life insurance is payable to beneficiaries—usually family members named by the person who passed away. This is most often payable in a lump sum.

Automobile insurance benefits

If the person was injured in a car crash, they will be entitled to *Statutory Accident Benefits*, often referred to as "no-fault benefits."

See Appendix A for a full listing of the benefits to which the injured person may be entitled. An experienced personal injury lawyer can assist you in completing the application materials for car insurance benefits.

Gathering and looking through these documents carefully will help you determine whether or not you are covered by insurance.

2. Takes Notes or Make a Diary for Future Litigation

With the emotional turmoil involved, even family members will be hard pressed to recall the events that happened following a traumatic event. Yet they can make notes, and diaries may be helpful for the purposes of any future lawsuit.

Important information to record might include:
- the dates of significant medical events—both good and bad—such as regaining consciousness, seizures, and surgeries;
- observations of the deficits, impairments, and challenges experienced by the injured person, including the dates and times these observations were made; and
- doctors' comments about the injuries, including any prognoses (predictions about the future outcome of an injury).

3. Take Photographs of the Injuries

Wounds heal and scars fade over time. Photographs of injuries, however, can be used later to bring to life the challenges you or your loved one faced in the days and weeks following the trauma.

Fast-forward your case four years down the road. A judge and a jury need to understand everything you or your loved one have been through. The injury photos you took will be invaluable at this point. As the saying goes, "A picture is worth a thousand words."

Scar and injury photographs can be used during future settlement discussions, mediations, pre-trial conferences, and trials. These events will be explained in detail in later chapters of this book.

4. Take Photographs of the Scene or Any Property Damage

If you think that someone might consider altering the scene of the injury following the event, it's a good idea to take some photographs right away. For example, if your wife suffered a severe ankle injury after falling on a poorly maintained walkway, take photographs of the area, just in case someone fixes the problem at some later time. Your photographs can serve to prove fault on behalf of the party responsible for maintaining the walkway.

Likewise, any warning signs or other evidence suggesting that the responsible party acknowledged the problem after the injury should be photographed. For example, in a case in which a heavy door malfunctioned and shattered someone's knee, the responsible party put up signs warning that the door was defective, and that it would be repaired shortly. Photographs of these signs could be very helpful in establishing fault.

Should an injury result in property damage (to a car or boat, for example), it is always helpful to have photographs of the damaged property. And the more photographs, the better. Photographs of the interior and exterior of the vehicle from different angles could be helpful to any accident reconstruction expert your lawyer might retain to investigate the case. While the police or insurance adjusters may also be taking photographs, they are looking at things from a different perspective, so it is good to have your own.

5. Keep all Receipts and Mileage Records

Keep a record of all of your out-of-pocket expenses arising from the injury. You and/or your family may be able to claim them in a future lawsuit, or through some form of insurance coverage. In particular, keep records and receipts from the following expenses:
- parking (from hospital parking lots or other medical facilities);
- meals purchased at the hospital;
- taxi or ambulance charges, as well as your own mileage records for travel to the hospital or other medical appointments;
- prescribed medications; and
- assistive devices (purchased or rented), including wheelchairs, scooters, walkers, canes, and braces.

6. Defer Speaking to an Insurance Adjuster Until After You Have Hired a Lawyer

Insurance company representatives (also referred to as *insurance adjusters*) may call you or your injured family member, seemingly out of the blue, following a serious personal injury. It may not even be clear whether they are from your own insurance company (if you have been in a car crash, for example) or from the at-fault party's insurance company. They will ask for details about the incident and the injuries, and they might even ask for a signed statement. Some insurance adjusters will actively try to dissuade an injured person or their family from hiring a lawyer. This is a self-serving practice that can leave vulnerable people at an extreme disadvantage down the line. Other insurance adjusters suggest that an injured person or a family member contact a personal injury lawyer. In any circumstance, it's important to be aware of your options and your rights.

My advice is simple: do not provide information to any insurance company representative until you have hired a lawyer. Making an insurance claim can be an uphill battle in which you and your future lawyer have to fight the insurance company for what is fair. You can protect yourself by having your lawyer handle discussions with the insurance company rather than doing this on your own. In the next chapter you'll learn how to choose the right lawyer for you.

TEGGART'S BOTTOM LINE

What to Do in the Days Following a Serious Personal Injury

Following an injury, there is a lot of time spent waiting around. Capable injured people or their family members can use this time productively. There are a number of things they can do to help start with preparation, including the following:

- Gather all insurance documents and benefits booklets.
- Take notes or keep a diary of important events following the injury.
- Take photographs of injuries, scarring, and bruising.
- Take photographs of the scene and any damaged property.
- Keep all receipts for injury-related expenses and keep a record of mileage travelled as well.
- Avoid speaking to any insurance company until you have spoken with an experienced personal injury lawyer.

CHAPTER TWO

Why Hire a Lawyer Early?

I suspect that for some of you, my telling you to hire a lawyer early after a serious personal injury or death of a loved one might come across as terribly self-serving. I get it. But truly, this is the best advice I can give you.

In this chapter, I will explain why it's important for seriously injured people and their families to consider hiring an experienced personal injury lawyer—sooner rather than later. In short, it's all about setting up for success in any future personal injury lawsuit. I can say with certainty that delays give insurance companies an advantage in the process.

1. Don't Miss Important Notice Periods

Depending on who the at-fault party is (a city, a municipality, or the Government of Ontario, for example), there may be important time limits by which an injured person, or the family of a deceased person, must notify the at-fault party of their intention to start a lawsuit. In some cases, the time period to notify the at-fault party of a potential lawsuit is less than two weeks!

Missing a notice period can be devastating to a claim for personal injury damages in a lawsuit. A court may throw out a case simply because the injured person didn't put the at-fault party on notice of a potential lawsuit in time.

Experienced personal injury lawyers are familiar with the relevant notice periods, whom they apply to, and how to comply with the law. These notice periods may or may not apply to your case. Make sure to find out and take appropriate action.

2. Don't Miss an Important Limitation Period

Generally speaking, there is a two-year limitation period for suing an at-fault party in a personal injury lawsuit in Ontario. That is, you must sue the at-fault party before the two-year anniversary of the event, or you will probably be barred from doing so.[2]

In the cases of children and people who do not have legal capacity, there are special rules that apply which extend the limitation period in certain circumstances. There are other exceptional circumstances in which the limitation period is extended—but these are few and far between. It's critical that you see an experienced personal injury lawyer as soon as possible after an event to understand and work

---

[2] As I write this, the Ontario government has suspended limitation periods retroactive to March 16, 2020 due to the Covid-19 virus outbreak. While I expect the government to eventually lift the suspension of limitation periods and return to the two year limitation period, we don't know yet how this will impact cases.

within the limitation period that applies to your case.

You may be thinking: "What's the big rush, if I have two years to sue?" Here's the thing: a personal injury lawyer will likely need medical records and other documents to start the lawsuit. It takes a lot of time to gather these documents and then draft the materials needed to begin the suit. Waiting puts you at risk of having your otherwise valid lawsuit thrown out because you did not act in time.

3. The Investigation Should Begin Immediately

In order to be successful in any future lawsuit, your lawyer will need to prove that someone other than you is at fault for your injuries. While the police or other officials may have investigated the incident leading to the injury or death, they will have approached the investigation from their own perspective, not yours. Information gathered in their investigation may not be very useful to you.

In order to prove fault in a personal injury case, investigators and forensic engineers may need to collect evidence as soon as possible after the incident has happened. Trained investigators may need to take statements. Forensic engineers may use special devices they have to measure everything from skid marks and sight lines to lighting levels. They may even download information from event data recorders, the "black boxes" of cars and trucks, to determine pre-incident speeds and braking and steering patterns.

The longer you wait to hire a lawyer, the more you risk the chance that the evidence will no longer be available. Vehicles with black boxes are sent to scrap yards and destroyed. A witness' memory fades or even worse—the witness disappears. Likewise, the scene of the incident may be altered in such a way that prevents engineers from performing an accurate forensic reconstruction of the event.

Hiring an experienced personal injury lawyer early will ensure that the incident is fully investigated while the evidence still exists and the memories of witnesses remain fresh. Moreover, it puts the lawyer in the best position to prove the case on the issue of fault in the future.

4. The Insurance Company Will Be Investigating Early

The vast majority of personal injury cases involve an insurance company. You may have to sue an individual person, but once they have been named, their insurance company steps in to defend them and pay for your losses if you are successful in the lawsuit.

Here is what you need to know about insurance companies: simply put, they are professional defendants. Every day they defend claims by injured people and their families. They have thousands of outstanding claims at any one time. They know the legal system well, and they know what needs to be done after a serious injury or death.

Insurance companies start their investigations as soon as they learn about a potentially serious personal injury or death claim against someone that they insured. They immediately appoint an insurance adjuster to begin investigating the claim. This person may begin by identifying and interviewing witnesses. They will hire private investigators to take photographs of the scene of the incident. Depending on the type of incident, they may retain their own forensic engineering company to begin some form of accident reconstruction.

Insurance adjusters will often attempt to contact and interview injured people and/or their family members. While these people are just doing their jobs, you should assume they are doing their best to find out information that will help their insurance company—and not the injured person and their family. To put it another way, if they can gather information from you that is damaging to your case, or the case of your loved one, it would be good for their insurance company.

Don't give the insurance company the advantage of a head start in this process. Protect your interests and hire an experienced personal injury lawyer early. They will investigate your case and will protect your interests. Should an insurance adjuster come calling, your lawyer will deal with them and you will avoid the risk of falling into the trap of providing them with potentially damaging information.

5. Waiting Delays Your Case and Makes You More Vulnerable During Settlement Negotiations

Depending on where a personal injury lawsuit is started, it can take anywhere from four to seven years to resolve it. In small cities, the timing will usually be somewhere near the lower end of this range, and in larger cities like Mississauga, Brampton, or Toronto, things will take longer.

Understandably, injured people and their families question why it takes so long to resolve a lawsuit. In fact, there are many reasons this is the case. Because of relatively recent case law from the Supreme Court of Canada, criminal cases take priority over personal injury cases in our court system. The system is bogged down with criminal cases and it can take years for a personal injury case to even get a trial date. Without a trial date, there is very little pressure on an insurance company to resolve a case.

Other factors also play a role in the length of time this process takes. First, personal injury lawyers need a realistic prognosis concerning a person's injuries before they can put a value on their case. It takes time for doctors to arrive at a prognosis. Second, scheduling time with lawyers can often be difficult as many of them are booked months in advance. This makes it difficult to schedule examinations for discovery, pre-trial conferences, and trials. Third, it will take some time for your personal injury lawyer to arrange for medical and other experts to assess you or your loved one.

Delays in hiring a lawyer simply prolong the time it will take for them to resolve your case. If financial resources are limited, injured people and their family members may find themselves in a vulnerable position during settlement negotiations. Just imagine what it would be like to have no money to pay the bills and then be offered a less-than-fair settlement from the insurance company. Your lawyer would likely tell you not to accept the offer, but you might be tempted to take it anyway, knowing that your credit cards were maxed out and that you were on the verge of declaring bankruptcy. You might imagine that with this settlement money, you could pay off your debts and maybe even have some cash left over. Feeling financially vulnerable, you might take the low-ball offer, despite your lawyer's advice.

Don't give an insurance company the advantage. Hire an experienced personal injury lawyer sooner rather than later.

In the next chapters you'll learn about some common obstacles to finding an experienced personal injury lawyer, and how to find the right lawyer for you or your family member.

TEGGART'S BOTTOM LINE

Why Hire a Lawyer Early?

- You set yourself or your family member up for success by hiring an experienced personal injury lawyer early.
- An experienced personal injury lawyer can deal with important notice periods that you can't afford to miss.
- An experienced personal injury lawyer will ensure that you don't miss the limitation period for suing an at-fault party.
- The investigation into the incident that caused the injury should start immediately, so investigators can interview witnesses and gather evidence before it is altered or destroyed.
- The insurance company will start investigating the incident right away. Don't give them the advantage of time and early preparation!
- Waiting to hire a lawyer will delay your being paid for your losses and may leave you financially vulnerable—and perhaps more likely to accept a settlement offer lower than you deserve.

CHAPTER THREE

Common Obstacles to Finding the Right Lawyer

Personal injury law is highly complex, and severely injured people and their families need to hire an experienced personal injury lawyer. Personal injury law is not an area of law that lends itself to someone representing themselves.

I understand, however, that many people are hesitant to contact a lawyer for a variety of reasons. In this chapter I will explain some common reasons people hesitate to reach out for this kind of professional help. Hopefully, after reading, you'll understand that there is very little risk in contacting an experienced personal injury lawyer. More importantly, you'll understand the benefit of hiring a lawyer to make sure your rights are protected.

1. "I Don't Know If I Need a Lawyer"

For most people, this experience may be their first foray into the legal world. In fact, they don't even know if they need a lawyer. A good rule of thumb to follow is that the more serious a person's injury, the more likely they will need an experienced personal injury lawyer to represent them.

Does this mean that a person with minor injuries shouldn't hire a lawyer? Not at all. What it does mean, however, is that the stakes are a lot higher for a seriously injured person than they are for a person with minor injuries. Financial costs can be insurmountable for seriously injured people or the family members of someone who dies through no fault of their own.

You may not know if you need a lawyer, but an experienced personal injury lawyer will be able to tell you if you do. And even if you feel that you may be partly at fault for your own injuries, I recommend that you contact a lawyer—especially if your injuries are serious. You may be able to recover money for your losses in a lawsuit even if you are partly at fault.

2. "I'm Not the Suing Type"

As Canadians, we view ourselves as very different from our American neighbours. Potential new clients frequently say to me, "I am not the suing type." I get it. Lawsuits are not pretty and dealing with lawyers and picking a fight with an insurance company can be scary when we hear stories in the media about how some insurers conduct their business.

The reality, however, is that some people have little choice. They may have been hit by a drunk driver and rendered a quadriplegic, with no ability to earn an income, pay for their care, or put food on the table. Another person may have suffered a severe knee injury, requiring reconstruction, and despite rehabilitation, will have to retire ten years earlier than they had expected because of the injury. A family may have lost one of its breadwinners and find themselves unable to cover the mortgage payment with just one income.

Personal injury law is all about levelling the playing field financially to recover the income a person will lose, and to pay for the care they will require in the future because of the injuries they have suffered. The unfortunate reality is that while you may not be the suing type, you owe it to yourself and your family to see a lawyer who will help you understand your rights when injuries impact you financially.

Just because you call an experienced personal injury lawyer doesn't mean you are stuck with them or even have to pursue a lawsuit. It is your decision whether or not to take legal action, and it's also up to you whether or not to hire the lawyer you have met with.

3. The Reputation of Personal Injury Lawyers

One of the main things people look for in personal injury lawyers is trustworthiness.

Having practiced personal injury law for over 22 years, I understand that my profession does not enjoy a stellar reputation. You have no idea how many personal injury lawyer jokes I have suffered through!

This reputation is no surprise to me. We are all judged by the lowest common denominator in our professions. Police officers are often pre-judged on the actions of the bad apples—not the heroes. And when we think of used car salesmen we leap to the notion of the fraudsters—not the salesperson who donates money to local charities and does their best to get you a good deal on your car purchase. To be honest, I do know of cases where personal injury lawyers reportedly have done things that back up the negative reputation we have. That said, most personal injury lawyers I know are dedicated to their jobs, do their best for injured clients, and take pride in their work and also in the excellent reputations they have earned in their communities.

4. "I Can't Afford a Lawyer"

Here is the good news. Despite lawyer advertising that makes it seem like an exceptional service, the vast majority of personal injury lawyers offer free consultations and don't charge a legal fee unless they recovery money for your losses.

This is called a *contingency fee*. Personal injury lawyers are not like real estate lawyers, who may require that you pay a certain amount up front before they start to work on your case. In fact, personal injury lawyers are the opposite. They do not charge a fee until the end of your case.

A contingency fee is a fancy way of saying that the lawyer charges a percentage of what they recover for your losses. The percentage varies from firm to firm, and most often sits in the range of 25 to 33 percent of your recovery. For example, in a 25 percent contingency fee agreement where the lawyer recovers $100,000 for your losses, the lawyer's fee would be $25,000.

5. "I Don't Want to Sue a Loved One Who Was at Fault for a Car Crash"

Often, particularly in car crash cases, the person responsible for injuring a person is a loved one. It could be a mother who lost control of her minivan while driving with an infant in the back seat. It could be a husband who drove through a red light while his wife sat in the passenger seat.

Injured people are concerned about suing a loved one for obvious reasons. They fear bankrupting the at-fault family member. They fear the push back from other family members. They fear the impact that a lawsuit may have on the insurance premiums the at-fault family member may have to pay in the future.

Here is the good news. While the lawsuit would have to be brought against the responsible family member, their car insurance will cover them up to the limits in the policy. In Ontario, all drivers are required to carry a minimum of $200,000 in what is called *liability insurance*. Liability insurance protects people in the event of a lawsuit after an accident that is their fault.

While the minimum available level of insurance is $200,000, the vast majority of Ontario drivers have $1,000,000 in liability insurance.

On top of this, car insurance policies and other insurance policies guarantee that the insurance company will hire and pay a lawyer to defend them in the lawsuit. This ensures they will not be out-of-pocket for any legal fees.

As far as a responsible loved one having to pay increased insurance premiums because of the car crash, this remains a possibility. That said, if you pay attention to your car insurance premiums, what I think you'll find is that they seem to increase every year even though you haven't been involved in a car crash. It's just the nature of car insurance. Insurers are in business to make money and they make more when they charge more. The bottom line is that the at-fault family member's insurance company is likely going to increase their insurance premiums regardless of whether they were responsible for the crash.

TEGGART'S BOTTOM LINE

Common Obstacles to Finding the Right Lawyer

- Call an experienced personal injury lawyer if you have been seriously injured, or if one of your loved ones has been seriously injured or killed.
- You may not know if you need a lawyer, but an experienced personal injury lawyer will be able to tell you if you do.
- You may feel that you are "not the suing type" but there are few risks to calling a lawyer and meeting with them to learn about your rights.
- Virtually all personal injury lawyers provide free consultations—you should not have to pay for this service.
- If you do choose to retain a lawyer, they will likely charge a contingency fee—a percentage of your financial recovery at the end of your case—and will not require any up-front payment.
- You may be entitled to money for your losses even though you are partly at fault for your injuries. An experienced personal injury lawyer can explain to you how fault can be divided between parties.
- Don't be dissuaded by the bad apples. Most professions have their bad apples, but experienced personal injury lawyers with excellent reputations have earned them by doing a good job for their clients.
- Don't be deterred by the possibility of having to sue a loved one who was responsible for your injuries. In all likelihood, an insurance company will be responsible for paying for your losses; it won't be your loved one who pays.

CHAPTER FOUR

How to Find the Right Personal Injury Lawyer

You know you need to meet with a personal injury lawyer, but who do you call? There is so much noise in the media about personal injury lawyers, it's hard to figure out which legal professional will be best able to help you.

In this chapter, you will learn important information about how personal injury lawyers are trained, the different types of personal injury law firms there are, and how to find and research personal injury lawyers. You'll also learn about some red flags; while some things you may find in your research that could be positive, others might not be so good. With this information, it's my hope that you can filter out the noise and find the right lawyer for you or your family member.

1. Training of Personal Injury Lawyers

You may have noticed that throughout this book I refer to "experienced personal injury lawyers." I do this on purpose, because someone doesn't become a personal injury lawyer simply by completing law school. This is something you need to know when looking for this kind of professional.

Let me start with a little background on lawyers and law firms, in the context of personal injury cases. The first thing you should know is that "personal injury law" isn't a course in most law schools. It is a highly specialized area of law that lawyers can only learn through working in a personal injury law firm.

The second thing you should know is that unlike medical doctors, law students learn very little about how to practice law in law school. For the most part, law school teaches critical thinking skills, how to understand case law and legal writing, and the basics about traditional areas of law, including, for example, contract, property, criminal, constitutional, corporate commercial, and family law. As students move through their three-year program, they can choose to take some more hands-on courses, in which they will learn more about the actual practice of law. These courses are relatively few and far between.

In my view, law schools need to collectively change the way they train lawyers. Some are beginning to, but it takes time to modify or even dispense with long-established traditions. Can you imagine going to an orthopaedic surgeon for a knee operation and finding out they were never actually taught how to do this procedure? The reality is that some lawyers who are graduating from law school with very little practical experience are putting out their shingles as personal injury lawyers.

When you begin your search for a personal injury lawyer following a serious injury or death, you need to make sure you find an experienced personal injury lawyer. In speaking with lawyers, be sure to ask how long they have been practicing personal injury law.

2. Personal Injury Law Firms 101

Personal injury law firms range from large-volume firms to smaller so-called boutique, firms. The large-volume firms that advertise in the media tend to take on many cases, no matter the severity of the injuries suffered. Generally, the smaller boutique personal injury firms tend to take on fewer cases, most of them serving clients with more severe injuries.

The next point you need to understand is that not all personal injury law firms practice in all areas of personal injury law. For example, in my firm, we focus on serious cases involving spinal cord injury, brain injury, complex orthopaedic injury, and fatal injury cases. Our clients have been injured in a wide variety of mishaps from car and motorcycle crashes to boating accidents to slip and falls, to product liability claims, to ATV accidents. If you have suffered a serious spinal cord injury, brain injury, or complex orthopaedic injury, then we may be the firm for you. If, however, you have suffered harm because a doctor has made a mistake, this is a case of medical malpractice—a specific kind of injury case that we do not take on for a variety of reasons.

Some firms restrict their practice to medical malpractice cases or slips and falls, choosing to focus on just one of these areas. Other firms take on just about every client who calls them.

When you are looking for a personal injury lawyer, it's important to understand what type of cases each firm accepts. The more time a firm spends on one specific type of personal injury case, the greater depth of understanding its lawyers are likely to have in this area—and the better they will be able to serve their clients.

3. How to Find a Personal Injury Lawyer

Following a serious personal injury, there are many ways to find a personal injury lawyer. There are literally hundreds of them practicing all over Ontario. You may even find that well-meaning people recommend lawyers to you. The question is whether the lawyer is right for you. It's only by doing your research that you can decide this for yourself. Some strategies you can use to find an experienced personal injury lawyer include the following:

A. *Google Searching*

A Google search is a good place to start, since almost every personal injury firm has a website. But this is only the beginning. Researching a firm's credentials is the most important part of your online research.

One thing to take into account in your Google search is whether or not the firm at the top of the page has paid to be there. Google allows you to buy advertisements, which can result in a top ranking. You will see beside the entry that this is an ad. Does this mean that you shouldn't research the firm? Not at all! It simply means that they have paid to be at the top of the Google search results.

B. Word of Mouth

Many well-meaning (and some not-so-well-meaning) people may recommend a lawyer to you. Friends and family are likely sincere in wanting to help you. I am, however, a little wary about referrals that come from tow truck drivers and even some health care providers. While these referrals may indeed be made in good faith, there is also the possibility that these people have some vested interest in your choosing a particular lawyer or firm. It's always best to do your own homework by researching a lawyer's credentials before making that first call.

4. How to Research Qualifications Online

A. Areas of Practice

First things first. As you review a lawyer's website, look to see if they restrict their practice to personal injury law. Does the lawyer or law firm represent insurance companies also? Do you want a lawyer who practices other areas of law? Do you want a lawyer or law firm that also represents insurance companies? These are the sorts of questions to ask yourself. It may be that the lawyer practices multiple areas of law and would do an excellent job for you, however, you need to ask yourself these questions.

Personal injury law is highly complex and it is difficult to just dabble in it. If a person has been seriously injured or killed, the financial consequences can be monumental, and it makes sense to work with an experienced personal injury lawyer.

What type of cases does the lawyer or law firm take on? I restrict my practice to brain injury, spinal cord injury, and complex orthopaedic injury cases, and I do not work in the area of medical malpractice. If someone has suffered whiplash, or another soft tissue injury, there are other lawyers out there who would be a better choice than me. Likewise, if you have a medical malpractice case, mine wouldn't be the law firm for you. There are firms that practice exclusively in this area that would serve you best.

B. *Former Client Reviews and Testimonials*

Former client reviews found on a law firm's website, its Google listing, or social media accounts can be helpful. What are people saying about the lawyer's services? What sorts of injuries or cases did these people have? Were any of the reviewer's injuries similar to your own situation?

In these days of online anonymity, it's important, sadly, to question whether the reviews and testimonials you read are legitimate. I am approached on a regular basis by companies who will guarantee me hundreds of positive Google reviews for a price. When I look for any service provider, I always keep this in mind. Take a look at the reviewer's profile. Are they real people? When I find that a reviewer is a family member of the service provider, or is otherwise linked in a way that might mean their viewpoint is not necessarily objective, I automatically cross them off my list.

A word of warning, though, about unfavourable reviews. Some people will write bad reviews for personal reasons that may have nothing to do with a service provider's performance. My firm recently received 4/5-star review on Google. The writer's name was not familiar to us, and it turned out that we had never had any dealings with him. We pride ourselves on the strength of our former client reviews so we dug deeper. What we found was that this person had reviewed 50 other businesses within the same hour in which he reviewed our law firm. It was clear that he was making an effort to increase his "local guide" status on Google, in order to qualify for perks that Google provides to people who review a lot of businesses.

Perhaps the best way to avoid the pitfalls of online reviews is to ask the law firm if they could give you the names of a few former clients who might be willing to speak with you about the service the firm provided. I've had numerous clients volunteer to provide these sorts of recommendations over the years. With their permission, I give potential clients their phone number, and the potential client can ask them any questions they want to ask about the work we did for them.

C. Social Media Accounts, Blog Posts, and Videos

Social media, blog posts, and videos can provide valuable information. Take a look at a potential firm's Facebook page, and read some of the interactions between the firm and its followers. Figure out for yourself if these seem genuine.

Videos can also provide helpful information. Some lawyers post videos of themselves talking about a particular issue in personal injury law. Even if that issue doesn't interest you, you may get a good sense of how that lawyer presents and whether or not they seem like a good authority in the area.

Many firms have blog posts on their website. Much like videos, blog posts can provide you with insights into the lawyer and the firm.

5. Red Flags

A. Solicitation Calls and Visits

I want to be really clear about this. If you or a family member have been seriously injured you should not be getting calls from personal injury law firms, or individuals you don't know, recommending a law firm, seemingly out of the blue. A little online research about a recent car crash and then a quick telephone directory search can lead someone with questionable motives right to you. It is against *the Rules of Professional Conduct* for lawyers to contact and solicit potential clients.

The same thing goes for unannounced hospital visits. You should be wary of lawyers or their representatives who show up unannounced in the hospital, wanting to meet with you or an injured loved one. The unfortunate reality is that hospitals are public spaces, and anyone can walk in and stroll around the hallways looking for seriously injured people and their families. This is a rather morbid thing to consider, but it does happen. To make matters worse, injured people and their families are in a vulnerable situation. The last thing they need is to be taken advantage of by someone unknown to them, who arrives on the scene looking for business.

B. Awards

When searching for personal injury lawyers online, you will find that some list awards they have received on their websites. I do this myself. I have been honoured to receive awards from third parties in acknowledgement of the service I have given to my clients, and I display these with pride.

You should be aware, though, that there are companies out there that are in the business of giving "awards"—and for a rather hefty fee. Every year I receive numerous e-mails from companies that have nominated me for—or actually granted me—one award or another. The catch is that they then want me to acknowledge that I would like to receive this so-called prestigious award, and pay a fee to get it. No fee, no award. It is outrageous to me that these bogus awards, which have nothing to do with service or performance, are so easy to acquire.

If you are seriously interested in a firm, take the time to look at the websites of any of the organizations that have given them awards, and see if you can figure out if the awards are truly legitimate.

C. Previous Judgments and Settlements

I'm not a huge fan of advertising previous cases' judgments and settlements. This is a common practice south of the border, and we have begun to see it in Ontario as well. My opinion is that every case is different, and just because a judgment or settlement was high, it doesn't necessarily mean that the lawyer did a good job. For example, a $1,000,000 settlement might seem impressive, however, if the case involved a child who was rendered a quadriplegic, then it is actually strikingly low.

The Law Society of Ontario (the province's governing body for lawyers) has special rules that apply to advertising by publicizing settlements or judgments. In my respectful opinion, I feel the rules do not help protect the consumer enough. Lawyers in Ontario are supposed to include a disclaimer when advertising judgments and settlements on promotional materials and websites. This disclaimer must tell readers that all cases are different, and that previous results don't necessarily reflect future results. This is all well and good, however, this disclaimer provides little protection to a potential client if it is buried somewhere in small font and lost in legalese. Moreover, the blinking neon tickertape of judgments and settlements scrolling across the top of the firm's website is no doubt going to attract far more attention, despite the fact that it may contain misleading information.

D. Other Patients in Hospitals

Other patients in the hospital will recommend their lawyer to newly injured people they meet. I have had clients who, during their lengthy hospital stays, have referred other patients they met to me. Happy with the service I was providing, they wanted to help out their friends by connecting them with me. I am aware, though, of a hospital referral story that has a rather dark side, and I mention this as a cautionary tale. Truthfully, I cannot determine whether this is true, or an urban myth, but since it does seem plausible, I have included it here.

The story I was told is that there was a law firm that actually paid actors to sit in a family room at a trauma centre in a Toronto hospital. Their job was to talk favourably about their (imaginary) lawyer in front of families of other injured people, in an effort to induce them to retain the firm. If this truly happened, it was a terrible scam. My advice is to be careful and do your research.

TEGGART'S BOTTOM LINE

How to Find the Right Personal Injury Lawyer

- Research the personal injury lawyer online and through word of mouth before contacting them.
- Look for the number of years of experience the lawyer has and keep in mind that Personal Injury Law is not a course taught in most law schools.
- Look for the type of personal injury law firm it is. Is it a volume-based law firm or a boutique law firm?
- Consider whether the lawyer restricts their practice to personal injury law or whether they practice other unrelated areas of law as well.
- Read former client reviews and testimonials with an eye for detail. Do they appear legitimate?
- Remember that a personal injury lawyer is prohibited from making unsolicited calls or visits by the **Rules of Professional Conduct.**
- Research the awards that a lawyer claims to have. Do these seem legitimate or do they appear to have been purchased?
- Be careful concerning the "tickertape" of former judgments or settlements. Out of context, or without your knowing the whole story, it's impossible to understand whether these do actually represent good results for the clients served.

CHAPTER FIVE

The First Meeting With a Personal Injury Lawyer

You've done your research, you've contacted an experienced personal injury lawyer, and you've made an appointment. So, what happens now?

In this chapter, you'll learn what you need to bring to your first meeting with a personal injury lawyer, what to expect from this meeting, and what factors to consider as you make a decision about hiring this person. You'll also learn how personal injury lawyers charge legal fees, and what a contingency fee retainer agreement is.

1. What Do I Need to Have With Me at the First Meeting?

It's always good to be prepared for the first meeting with a lawyer. Many people find that they are nervous and a bit intimidated. This is entirely normal, but making sure you are prepared ahead of time will help prevent your nerves from getting the better of you during the meeting.

Whether the first meeting is at the lawyer's office, your home, or in the hospital, there are some items you should have on hand for the lawyer to review. These include the following:

- all relevant insurance documents (benefits booklets, information sheets, or statements, for example);
- any readily available medical reports;
- photographs of the injuries (these may be on your phone);
- contact information for anyone who saw the incident happen;
- photographs of the scene or property damage;
- any contact information for the investigating officer, or police reports if there was an investigation;
- contact information for any insurance adjuster who has attempted to speak with you or your injured family member;
- your own photo identification, since lawyers are required to take copies of this for their clients; and
- a pen and some paper or an electronic device to make note of any important information you want to record.

Often clients create a list of questions they have and bring these to the first meeting. This can be very helpful; not only does it ensure that they get all the information they need, but it also helps them get a feel for the way the lawyer communicates with them and handles their concerns.

2. How Long Will the Meeting Last?

This is a tough one to answer because every case is different. I would estimate that my average first meeting with a potential client lasts approximately an hour and a half.

I often attend initial meetings at the hospital, and I try to limit these to 30 - 45 minutes, depending on the person's impairments. I am aware that my potential client may be on pain medication, may be suffering from fatigue or confusion, and as a result, may have a limited attention span. The last thing I want to do is tire this person out or overload them with too much information. In these circumstances, I will usually follow up by meeting with the injured person's family members or arranging a second meeting with the injured person at a later date.

3. Solicitor-Client Confidentiality

It can be uncomfortable meeting a lawyer for the first time. You may be asked to talk about personal health or family issues. Discussing these things with a stranger can be unnerving.

While it may be only a small consolation, you should know that your communications with the lawyer are protected by what lawyers refer to as *solicitor-client privilege*. This means that the lawyer must keep all your communications confidential unless you instruct them otherwise. This is one of our most important rules, and lawyers take it very seriously. You may take some peace of mind from the fact that everything you tell your lawyer will be kept in strict confidence.

4. What Issues Will the Lawyer Cover in the Meeting?

The lawyer will cover a range of topics during a first interview. While every lawyer and every case are different, there is some basic information that the lawyer will need to learn. I usually ask for the following:

- basic background information, including things like age, education, and employment history;
- details of the person's pre-injury health;
- details of the person's pre-injury income (for adults) or education (for children);
- details of the injuries suffered, treatment, surgery, and testing performed; and
- details of how and when the injury happened.

I also provide information that includes:
- the definition of personal injury law, including the concepts of negligence, causation, and damages (explained further in Chapter 7);
- my recommendation as to whether to pursue a case, or whether there are other options in the current situation;
- an explanation of contingency fee retainer agreements and how they work;
- my qualifications and details about my law firm;
- a warning about the dangers of social media usage and surveillance (explained further in Chapter 6);
- the anticipated timeline for the case, including the steps involved; and
- my suggested next steps in the process.

5. The Contingency Fee Retainer Agreement

A. *General Information*

One of the most important things an experienced personal injury lawyer will discuss with you in your first meeting is the way in which they will be paid. While there may still be lawyers out there charging an hourly rate for their services, the vast majority of experienced personal injury lawyers charge a fee based on a percentage of the amount that they recover for their clients. This is referred to as a *contingency fee* because the fee depends (or is contingent) upon the value of the person's case. The agreement a client signs with their personal injury lawyer is therefore called a *contingency fee retainer agreement*.

Historically, lawyers were not allowed to charge contingency fees, however, over the last 20 years, Ontario's courts and legal organizations have accepted them as a fair and workable billing system.

At the time of the writing of this book, the Ontario Government has recently proposed changes to the *Solicitors Act* regulations which have yet to be proclaimed into force. Should these amendments be proclaimed, the changes would likely impact the standard form of contingency fee retainer agreements, the advertisement of fees, and the treatment of costs and disbursements. *Costs*, in the legal context, refers to an amount paid by the at-fault party's insurance company. This amount is meant to reimburse the injured person for a portion of their legal fees following a successful settlement or judgment. *Disbursements* refers to the amount of money a lawyer spends in building a case. This could include fees for hospital, employment, or income tax records, police records, clinical notes and records of healthcare providers, and other expert reports, among other things. There is no predicting how the Government will deal with these issues and I encourage readers to speak with their lawyers regarding the form of contingency fee agreement they may be proposing.

A contingency fee retainer agreement provides an injured person and their family members access to legal services they might not otherwise be able to afford. Many refer to this as *access to justice*. The lawyer takes the risk of not being paid, in favour of charging a percentage of the person's financial recovery in a lawsuit. The client, on the other hand, doesn't have to pay legal fees up front.

A contingency fee retainer agreement makes sense in personal injury cases. Many injured people and the families of those who have passed away are in a difficult financial situation. Injured people are often unable to work because of their injuries and impairments. The families of those who have died in some sort of mishap, are potentially without the income the deceased person would have contributed for years to come. I would hazard a guess that very few people would have access to justice in personal injury cases were it not for contingency fee retainer agreements.

So, how do these agreements work? While each contingency fee retainer agreement is different,[3] they generally have a number of things in common:

- The client does not have to pay any legal fees up front.
- The lawyer charges a legal fee when the case resolves through settlement or judgment.
- The legal fee is a percentage of the client's settlement or judgment.
- The lawyer will pay disbursements up front.
- The client will get to keep any amount paid for costs.

---

3 This is subject to the Ontario Government's proclaiming changes to the *Solicitors Act* regulations in the future that may dictate a standard form contingency fee retainer agreement.

B. How a Typical Contingency Fee Retainer Agreement Works

Let me use a hypothetical example to show you how a typical contingency fee retainer agreement might work.

Joe is injured in a car crash. His lawyer charges a contingency fee of 30 percent. The insurance company for the at-fault driver settles the case with Joe for $100,000 plus costs in the amount of $15,000, and disbursements in the amount of $10,000.

For cases brought under the new *Simplified Procedure* rules (which apply to cases worth less than $200,000), the maximum amount payable for costs is $50,000.

If Joe's lawyer is successful at trial, the insurance company for the at-fault driver will pay for most, if not all, of the disbursements. As the lawyer has already paid this money to pursue Joe's claims, the entire amount of the disbursements will be repaid to the lawyer once the case has been settled.

For cases brought under the new Simplified Procedure rules noted above, the maximum payable for disbursements is $25,000.

Here are the calculations of how much Joe and his lawyer would recover in this example:

Legal fee: 30% of $100,000	$30,000
HST (13%) on legal fee	$3,900
Total Legal Fee (including HST)	$33,900

Joe's settlement	$100,000
Costs	$15,000
Disbursements	$10,000
Total paid by insurer	$125,000

Joe's net recovery after legal fees:
$100,000 - $33,900 (legal fee, including HST) + $15,000 (costs) = $81,100

Joe's lawyer will be paid:
$30,000 (legal fee) + $3,900 (HST) + $10,000 (disbursements) = $43,900

C. Typical Percentages Lawyers Charge in Contingency Fee Retainer Agreements

The percentage charged by a lawyer under a contingency fee retainer agreement should be determined with a number of factors in mind. These factors include the nature and complexity of the case, the risks involved, the amount of time the lawyer dedicates to the case, and the result that the lawyer achieves for the client.

Lawyers will most often charge an amount in the range of 25 to 33 percent of the client's financial recovery. That said, having taken over a number of cases from other firms, I have seen contingency fee retainer agreements in which lawyers have intended to charge as much as 40 percent of the client's financial recovery. With all due respect to my colleagues, my opinion is that a retainer agreement with a fee of 35 percent or more is inappropriate.

D. *The Contingency Fee Retainer Agreement: A Cautionary Note*

Ultimately, the terms of your contractual relationship with the personal injury lawyer you hire will be defined in a written contingency fee retainer agreement. A word of warning: this agreement will be lengthy and will detail all aspects of your business dealings with the lawyer, including the percentage the lawyer charges. Every contingency fee retainer agreement is different.[4] I cannot stress strongly enough that you should read the full agreement and make sure your lawyer answers any questions you may have about it before you sign.

6. What Won't Be Covered in Your First Meeting?

From time to time, potential new clients want a lawyer's assessment of how much their case is worth in the first meeting. While it might be tempting for some lawyers to suggest an amount that impresses the client (and increases their chance of being hired, perhaps), my own practice is not to give any assessment of the value of the case in the first meeting. With so many unanswered questions at this point, I feel it is impossible to guess at a fair value, and frankly, I believe it is inappropriate to do so in most cases.

One critical question right at the start should be whether or not the incident happened as the injured person remembers it. Often, my brain-injured clients are unable to recall exactly what occurred.

---

4   *Ibid.*

It will only be after a thorough investigation that we will have a complete and accurate picture of the event. As you might expect, the person's medical prognosis will play a role in the valuation of the case, and it is premature to know what this may be. They may require knee replacement surgery followed by years of costly rehabilitation in the future, however, doctors will not know this for some time. In addition, we don't yet have the full details of what the injured person's financial losses are likely to be. Will they return to work in the future? Will they have to retire early because of their injuries? Finally, we won't know the extent of the injured person's future care needs at this early stage. It is only over time that the picture becomes clearer.

7. How Do I Decide Whether to Hire the Lawyer?

Assuming the lawyer recommends moving ahead with your case, you will need to decide whether you wish to hire this person.

At the first meeting with a lawyer, clients often experience a bit of information overload, so don't feel pressure to make a decision right then and there. While you certainly may make a decision if you like, you may also ask to take some time to think about it. You might even opt to interview another personal injury lawyer, if you think a second opinion might be helpful. Remember, you are in charge and you shouldn't feel forced into retaining a lawyer. Nor should you feel obligated to commit because this person has gone to the trouble of coming to see you.

By hiring a personal injury lawyer, you are basically contracting into a relationship, just as you would with a carpenter or a dentist.

As in every relationship, "fit" is important. You are signing up for what could be a very lengthy process. It's important that you assess your comfort level with the lawyer you are considering hiring, and whether you feel confident that you can trust this person to do their best for you. The trust element is a difficult thing to figure out in an interview. As the saying goes, "Trust is something you earn."

So how can a lawyer earn your trust in that first interview? The reality is that you just can't be completely certain, but there are some things that you can look for that may give you a good indication of trustworthiness. Here are some questions to consider:

- Did the lawyer show up on time for your meeting?
- What level of experience does the lawyer have with personal injury cases like yours?
- What percentage does the lawyer charge under their contingency fee retainer agreement?
- Was the lawyer well prepared for your meeting, having reviewed the information you provided in your initial telephone call—or were they disorganized and foggy on your details?
- Did the lawyer listen to you?
- Did the lawyer give you their undivided attention, or were they taking calls or answering e-mails during your meeting?
- Did the lawyer explain things in a way you could understand?
- Did the lawyer give you an opportunity to ask questions, and did they answer these clearly?
- Did you actually meet with the lawyer who will be handling your case, or did they send a paralegal or another representative in their place?
- Did the lawyer provide you with a list of options or a potential

plan to bring your case to a successful resolution?

Some of these issues may be a big deal to some people and not so much to others. My advice is to remember that in any relationship, the small things that bother you at the beginning often snowball and bother you more over time. Pay attention to your feelings and trust your intuition during the time you first spend with a lawyer.

8. What If I Want to Fire My Personal Injury Lawyer?

Unfortunately, not all relationships with personal injury lawyers go well. An injured person or their family may hire a lawyer to handle their case. Somewhere down the line they realize that this is not the lawyer for them.

Over the years, I have taken over on many cases with clients who were unhappy with their previous personal injury lawyer. The complaint that I have heard most often is that the lawyer or the staff at the firm did not return phone calls or e-mails. In many cases, injured people or their family members had no idea what was happening with their cases. In a situation like this, in which there has been an obvious communication breakdown, it is understandable for a client to feel that trust has been breached, and that they want to end the relationship.

In circumstances like these, the injured person is entitled to retain another personal injury lawyer to take over their case. It is a fairly simple transaction in which the former lawyer sends the file to the new lawyer. The lawyers handle the transaction in its entirety and the injured person doesn't have to call and "dump" their former lawyer. The injured person doesn't have to pay their former lawyer's bill either. Instead, the new lawyer agrees to pay the bill out of the fee that they charge at the end of the case.

TEGGART'S BOTTOM LINE

The First Meeting with a Personal Injury Lawyer

- Come prepared for your first meeting with a personal injury lawyer. Bring relevant insurance documents, photographs, police reports, and a pen and paper. In advance of the meeting, write down any questions you want to ask.
- Your conversation with the lawyer will be confidential.
- Lawyers will cover many issues in the first meeting including, your background, how the injury happened, the legal principles of **negligence** and **damages,** and whether or not you should pursue a lawsuit for personal injury damages.
- The lawyer should also let you know how much they intend to charge under a contingency fee retainer agreement. Typically, lawyers charge between 25 and 33 percent of the person's financial recovery, depending on numerous factors, including the complexity of the case, the anticipated amount of work, the risks in the case, and the financial result anticipated.
- Read the Contingency Fee Retainer Agreement and ensure that all your questions are answered before signing it.
- Don't expect the lawyer to tell you how much your case is worth in the first meeting.
- Deciding on whether to retain a new lawyer can be difficult. As in every relationship, "fit" is important. You always have the option to interview more than one personal injury lawyer before deciding which one to retain.
- You can fire your personal injury lawyer if you are unhappy with their service. Ideally, though, you'll be able to make an informed decision at the start.

CHAPTER SIX

Dangers of Social Media Accounts, Surveillance, and the Importance of Confidentiality

Another important topic that I usually discuss in the first meeting with a potential new client is the danger that comes with social media use and surveillance. I've dedicated an entire chapter—albeit a short one—to this issue, because I feel it is vitally important in today's world.

In this chapter, you will learn about the dangers of social media use and insurance company surveillance to those involved in a lawsuit. You'll also learn about the risks of discussing your case with the healthcare providers who are working with you.

1. Dangers of Social Media Use

As soon as an insurance company learns of your intention to bring a claim (and sometimes even before), they will begin to try to dig up dirt on you. Given the easy access of social media, they often begin with Google, and follow up by looking at your online profiles—Facebook, Instagram, Twitter, etc. It's inexpensive to seek information in these places, and insurers are well aware that many people post about their injuries online.

In my first meeting with a new client or their family members, I warn them of this danger and recommend that they do not post anything related to their situation on social media until the case has been officially settled.

This is because over the past ten years, courts have decided that an injured person's social media accounts are fair game for insurance companies. While there is case law on both sides, many courts have ordered an injured person to allow open access to their social media accounts for the insurance company representing the responsible party. There is a real risk that a judge will put privacy matters aside and open your online accounts to scrutiny of the insurance company and the court deciding your case.

As you read this, you may be thinking that you don't care, or that you don't post a lot on social media, so you have nothing to worry about. Insurance company defence lawyers are highly motivated to find that one photo, post, or negative word that can be used against you, and they will pore over your social media accounts in an effort to find it.

You may feel certain that your posts are harmless, but in the context of a personal injury lawsuit, they may actually contribute in some way to a negative outcome.

Here's an example: At some point during your lawsuit you will be asked to give a sworn statement at *examinations for discovery* (see Chapter 9). At this time, the insurance company lawyer will ask you lots of questions about the things that you are able to do and unable to do. They may ask you whether you are able to walk without your cane. You tell the lawyer that you cannot. The insurance company does its homework, and finds on your social media account a photo or even a short video clip of you on your feet, dancing at your sister's wedding. It may be that you temporarily ditched your cane and suffered the painful consequences later, but the image doesn't tell that part of the story. The defence lawyer will use it to attack your future credibility, suggesting that anything you say may not be believable. Personal injury cases are all about whether a person is believable and, in this instance, a two-minute dance without your cane and a social media post may have damaged your case terribly.

There are so many examples like this in case law today. Don't shoot yourself in the foot, so to speak. Take a self-imposed break from social media. It's the best way to ensure your privacy during the legal process.

2. Dangers of Insurance Company Surveillance

It may surprise you to learn that many insurance companies conduct surveillance.

This is usually done by private investigators paid by the insurance company. You may spot them in vans or other vehicles, often with tinted windows, sitting outside your residence. They follow you around with a digital camera, taking video and photographs in an effort to catch you in a "gotcha" moment. Or they might try another tactic—taking days of video in an effort to make it look as if the injured person's impairments aren't really that severe.

Later, the surveillance video and photographs could be used against you. They could be presented at trial or be provided to defence medical experts in an effort to undermine your case.

Sometimes investigators are inconspicuous, and clients don't notice them. Other times they are entirely obvious. It could be that they are just bad at their jobs, but I sometimes wonder if they have intentionally shown themselves to the injured person just to upset them. These people could be male or female, and they may use many different methods of surveillance. In addition to digging up dirt about you online, they may follow you in a vehicle or on foot, with hidden cameras at the ready.

Many clients find it a terribly unnerving invasion of privacy, being followed around by a private investigator. This is entirely understandable. And while surveillance can be very annoying to the person being watched, it is not an illegal thing to do. Some might take down license plate numbers and report them to the police. The local police service will usually contact the person, determine that they are a private investigator, advise the injured person that this is the case, and leave it at that. It is probably a good idea to contact the police if you are concerned at any point.

There is really very little you can do to stop surveillance from happening. Unfortunately, it is just part of the price you pay for entering the world of personal injury law.

3. Risks of Discussing Your Case with Healthcare Providers

Over the years, I have seen many people damage their own case by discussing it with others. Most often, they shared legal advice their lawyer had given them with friends and healthcare providers.

Please do not discuss your case—or the advice your lawyer gives you—with others, especially your healthcare providers!

Discussing your case with healthcare providers is dangerous because there is a risk that the information will end up in the hands of the insurance defence lawyer. Healthcare providers have an obligation to take notes. Their notes make up part of their clinical file about you. Your lawyer is probably going to have to request and then provide your healthcare providers' clinical notes and records to the insurance defence lawyer as part of the documentary discovery process you'll learn about in chapter 9. This means that the confidential legal advice your lawyer gave you would end up in the hands of your opponent in the case: the insurance defence lawyer! Don't give them this advantage. You may be spending a great deal of time with some kind and caring healthcare workers. It may be very tempting to share your personal information with them. The only way to ensure your privacy though, is to keep your case-related information to yourself.

There is another reason not to discuss your case with others. Over the years, I have seen numerous clients taken advantage of by so-called friends who have less-than-good intentions. They learn about your lawsuit and all of a sudden, they are coming to you for a handout or fashioning a scheme to access your money at the end of the case.

Injured people are sometimes physically, cognitively, or psychologically vulnerable. They may not even realize they are being duped until it is too late. All the more reason not to discuss your case with anyone. I wish I didn't have to give you this advice, but this is the harsh reality of the world we live in.

TEGGART'S BOTTOM LINE

Dangers of Social Medica Accounts, Surveillance, and the Importance of Confidentiality

- Don't post anything on social media until your case has been resolved!
- A court may order you to produce a record of all of your social media posts. Your privacy can be limited once you begin a lawsuit.
- You may think that your social media posts won't hurt your case, but you are not in a good position to assess this. Don't take the risk.
- Your credibility is at issue in a lawsuit. Insurance defence lawyers will do everything they can to use your social media posts to hurt your case and attack your credibility. Don't make it harder on yourself (and on your lawyer) by posting on social media.
- Watch out for private investigators sitting outside your home with cameras and video equipment. They will usually be in vehicles with tinted windows, and may follow you around looking for a **gotcha** moment.
- The insurance defence lawyer can use any video surveillance or photographs they have to undermine your case.
- Contact the police if you are concerned about a stranger taking photos or following you.
- Don't discuss your case or the legal advice you have received with your healthcare providers or others. This information may end up in the hands of the insurance defence lawyer. It also creates the risk of less-than-well-intentioned "friends" coming up with a scheme to access your money at the end of the case.

CHAPTER SEVEN

Personal Injury Law 101: What You Need to Know

You hire a lawyer to fight for your rights, argue your case, and secure a settlement or judgment to ensure that you have the money to pay for your losses. Even with this expert involved, it helps to understand some of the basic concepts at play in a lawsuit.

Generally speaking, in order to recover money in a lawsuit, a lawyer has to prove three things: (1) that someone other than their client was at fault, (2) that the other person caused an injury, and (3) that the injured person suffered *damages*.

The case must be proven on what is called a *balance of probabilities*. Personal injury lawsuits are civil cases, not criminal cases. While in criminal cases, crown attorneys are required to prove their case "beyond a reasonable doubt," the standard of proof is lower in civil cases. To win a civil case, an injured person simply has to prove that their case is more likely than the defence case. A visual way to understand the civil standard is to imagine the scales of justice. An injured person wins their case if the scale tips just 51% in their favour. To use a hockey analogy, you don't have to win the game 5-0, you just have to win the game 3-2[5].

This chapter is all about the way the law works, as it relates to personal injury lawsuits. You'll learn about the issues of liability, causation, and damages. Once you understand these important issues, you will also understand how personal injury lawyers determine the value of a case.

1. Liability

A. Who Is at Fault?

When lawyers talk about liability, what they are really talking about is fault. Who was at fault for the person's injuries? Usually fault is found where someone's actions fell below the standard of care that we expect from a reasonable person. Falling below this standard is referred to as *negligence*.

Negligence is one of a number of wrongful acts that lawyers refer to as *torts*. Because of this, lawyers will often refer to an injured person's case as their *tort case*. Lawyers refer to the person who committed the wrongful act as the *tortfeasor*.

I'll give a few examples of ways in which a lawyer can prove negligence in a personal injury case.

In a car crash case, if a lawyer can prove someone is driving down the road in their car and they fail to stop at a stop light, they will be found negligent. In other words, the ordinary and reasonable

---

5   Thanks to my colleague, fellow personal injury lawyer Mike Smitiuch, for this great analogy that he has used in numerous jury trials.

person would have stopped at the stop light. The driver will be found negligent because they did not stop. In this instance they will have committed a tort or a civil wrong.

It's important to point out that a lawyer must prove negligence, or the injured person will not recover any money for their losses. For example, if someone is drinking all night at home and becomes intoxicated, gets into his truck and slams it into a telephone pole, suffering brain damage as a result, barring other exceptional factors, he probably will not have a tort case. This is because the lawyer cannot prove that anyone other than the now brain-damaged drunk driver was negligent. He consumed alcohol at home, chose to get into his truck, and slammed into a telephone pole. He is the only person at fault.

B. Contributory Negligence: Was the Injured Person Also at Fault?

In some cases, a court will find that the injured person is partly to blame for their own injuries. This is referred to as *contributory negligence*. Here's an example: Cheryl is walking down a city sidewalk at night. She is not paying attention and slips and falls on ice and breaks her neck. In this instance, a court may find that Cheryl is 25 percent contributorily negligent for not paying attention to where she was walking, and the city is deemed to be 75 percent responsible for failing to put down salt or sand on the sidewalk, which created a hazard. Lawyers refer to this dividing of responsibility as *apportionment of liability*. (Lawyers really do have a knack for coming up with complicated terms!)

Here is the thing about contributory negligence, from the perspective of the injured person: the court will reduce the injured person's money and other losses (also referred to as damages) by whatever percentage of fault is their own. In the example above, if Cheryl is found to be 25 percent contributorily negligent and a court found her losses to be worth $1,000,000, this amount would be reduced by 25 percent ($250,000 in this case) to account for Cheryl's own degree of fault. The city would then be responsible for paying the remaining $750,000 for the percentage of fault attributed to it.

C. What If More Than One Party Is at Fault?

Courts will also divide fault if there is more than one party responsible for the person's injuries. For example, consider the example of a boater speeding down the lake at night. His boat slams into a sailboat that didn't have its navigational lights activated, and a passenger is injured. In this scenario, a court may divide fault (or apportion liability) between the speeding boater and the sailboat captain who didn't display his navigational lights.

Much like the way in which courts deal with contributory negligence, a court would assign a percentage of fault to each party. For example, a court might find that the speeding boater was 75 percent at fault and the sailboat operator was 25 percent at fault. In this instance, the insurance company for the speeding boater would be responsible for paying 75 percent of the injured person's losses. The insurance company for the sailboat operator would be responsible for paying the remaining 25 percent.

2. Damages: The Value of Your Case

In personal injury law, *damages* refers to the money paid to a person who was injured or suffered a loss because of another person's wrongful act. Damages are divided into different "pots"[6] that might apply to a particular case. In legal terms these different pots of money are referred to as *heads of damages*.

In what follows, I will describe the most common heads of damages that make up a person's damages in a personal injury case.

A. Loss of Income/Earning Capacity and Pension Losses

An injured person who suffers a loss of past income and maybe also a loss of the future ability to earn an income because of someone's wrongful act may be entitled to payment for these losses.

Damages for past loss of income are relatively straightforward.[7] This is the income that a person has lost (due to their injuries) between the time they were injured and the date of their trial.

Loss of future earning capacity can be a bit more complicated. It is the difference between the income a person would have earned (had it not been for their injuries) and the income they earn (if any) after their injuries. It could be that the injured person will suffer a loss of earning capacity because they will never work again, will only be able to take on part-time work, or will have to retire early because of their injuries. Likewise, it may be that the injured person returns to work but in a different job (that they can handle with their disability) and earns less income as a result.

An experienced personal injury lawyer will usually hire a forensic accountant or an economist to calculate the present value of an

---

6 I acknowledge my legal mentor, Roger Oatley with this apt description of the different categories of damages.
7 In car crash cases, an injured person is only entitled to 70 percent of their pre-collision income up to the date of the trial under Ontario law.

injured person's future loss of earning capacity.

If a person cannot work because of their injuries, they may also be forced to accept a lesser pension because their injuries kept them from contributing to their pension plan. In this instance, the person may be able to recovery money for their pension losses. A forensic accountant or economist will usually calculate these losses as well.

B. Care Costs

The unfortunate reality is that most severely injured people will require care above and beyond what is covered by OHIP.[8] While the initial hospital stay will be covered, many medical expenses incurred after discharge from hospital will not be covered. An injured person may be entitled to recover money to pay for the past and future care costs that are not covered by OHIP.

Typical examples of medical and rehabilitation costs that are not covered by OHIP include the following healthcare services:
- occupational therapy,
- speech language pathology,
- physiotherapy,
- massage therapy,
- psychology or social work,
- rehabilitation support, and
- personal support.

---

8 OHIP has what is called a *subrogated interest* in cases not involving a car crash. This means that OHIP can recover the costs of the services for treatment of the injured person if fault can be established against another party.

In addition to these services, injured people may be entitled to recover the cost of certain devices and accommodations including:
- vehicle modifications,
- home modifications,
- medications and medical supplies (catheters, for example),
- assistive devices (including equipment like scooters, wheelchairs, walkers, canes), and
- high-tech prosthetics.

An experienced personal injury lawyer will usually hire experts to assess an injured person's future care needs. They will prepare a report outlining their opinion, and the lawyer will then send this report to a forensic accountant or economist to calculate the present value of the injured person's future care costs.

When you read about multi-million-dollar verdicts in our media, more often than not, the lion's share of the money an injured person recovers for their losses is linked to these sorts of medical and rehabilitation expenses.

C. Housekeeping and Maintenance Expenses

If an injured person has paid or will have to pay someone to perform housekeeping and home maintenance tasks because they cannot do these themselves due to their injuries, then they may be entitled to payment for the cost of these services. The injured person can therefore recover money for their past expenses and also receive money for their projected future expenses. The projection of these future expenses is known as a "loss of housekeeping and home maintenance capacity."

As an example, a person may have to hire someone to cut their lawn or shovel their driveway. They may need assistance with chores such as heavy outdoor or indoor cleaning. The injured person may be entitled to recover money for these expenses in a personal injury lawsuit.

An experienced personal injury lawyer will usually rely on expert opinions to project the injured person's housekeeping and home maintenance needs. As with loss of earning capacity, the lawyer will send the experts' opinions to a forensic accountant or economist to calculate the present value of the injured person's future loss of housekeeping and home maintenance capacity.

D. General Damages for Pain and Suffering

A person injured by the wrongful act of another may be entitled to money damages for their pain and suffering and loss of enjoyment of life. Lawyers refer to damages for pain and suffering as *non-pecuniary damages*.

Pain and suffering and loss of enjoyment of life is usually the most misunderstood head of damages. I suspect this is due to the influence of American legal reporting on our culture. In the US, different states have different rules and case law concerning damages for pain and suffering and loss of enjoyment of life. In some states there are caps on general damages while in others there are no caps.

In Canada, the Supreme Court capped the maximum amount an injured person can recover for pain and suffering in 1978.[9] In 1978 dollars, this cap was $100,000. Accounting for inflation, the current

---

9 *Andrews et al v. Grand & Toy Alberta Ltd. et al*, [1978] 2 S.C.R. 229.

cap on general damages for pain and suffering is approximately $389,744.[10] This cap is meant to be the upper limit, reserved for the most serious of cases such as a child who was severely injured and will have very little quality of life for a lengthy period of time.

What courts try to do when assessing damages for pain and suffering, is to put the person's injuries on a scale from $0-$389,744.[11] Judges use past cases involving similar injuries as a measuring stick or precedent to establish some level of consistency. In jury cases, sometimes the jury is told of the cap and in other cases it is not. This can create situations in which the jury awards pain and suffering damages that differ greatly from those judges have previously awarded in similar cases.

Recently, there has been discussion concerning the elimination of the cap on general damages. Only time will tell if this actually happens.

E. Out-of-Pocket Expenses

An injured person may be entitled to payment on account of the out-of-pocket expenses they have incurred because of their injuries. Examples of typical out-of-pocket expenses include mileage expenses, parking expenses, and other related expenses that do not fall under one of these categories.

---

10 This is the January, 2020 cap.
11 While beyond the scope of this book, I want to point out that in car crash cases a statutory deductible applies to awards for pain and suffering in some cases. In these cases, if a court assesses general damages to be less than $131,854 then it will reduce the award by a statutory deductible of $39,556. This is the January, 2020 deductible; however, this amount increases each year.

F. *Family Law Act* Claims

Family members of people who are injured or killed due to the negligence of another may be entitled to be paid for their losses. Under the *Family Law Act*,[12] family members may be entitled to damages for the loss of the injured person's "care, guidance, and companionship." That is, the care, guidance, and companionship that the injured or deceased person would have provided to their family member had it not been for their injuries or death.[13]

Family members of injured people, or people who have died, are also entitled to recover their financial losses in a lawsuit against the responsible party. For example, loss of income, funeral expenses, loss of shared family income (the income the deceased person might have brought into the family), and out-of-pocket expenses may be payable to the family members of the person who was injured or killed.

It is important to point out that in fatal injury cases, the court is entitled to assess whether the deceased was contributorily negligent. That is, whether the deceased was at fault in any way for their own death. Any fault attributed to the deceased will flow through to their family members making a claim under the *Family Law Act*. For example, if the court finds that the deceased was 40 percent at fault, their family members' damages will be reduced by 40 percent.

---

12 R.S.O. 1990, c. F. 3 at s. 61.
13 While beyond the scope of this book, I want to point out that in car crash cases a statutory deductible may apply to the claims of family members of injured people. In these cases, if the damages award is $65,926 or less, the court will reduce the award by a deductible of $19,778. (These figures are the amounts for January, 2020.) The deductible does not apply to fatal injury cases.

G. Punitive Damages

Punitive damages are the amount of money payable by an at-fault party because of their outrageous conduct. In instances, where conduct is deemed outrageous, a court may order punitive damages to punish the party and to deter others from doing the same thing.

I've included punitive damages because we read about them from time to time, particularly in American media reports. The reality, however, is that punitive damages are rarely awarded in Ontario. Because courts will be called on to consider previous punishment already received for the conduct (e.g., criminal penalties like jail time or a fine), awards are typically modest in Ontario, unlike in some areas of the United States.

3. Causation: Did the Person Cause Your Injury?

In order to prove causation, it must be determined that the conduct of the at-fault party cause or led to the damages the injured person is claiming in a lawsuit.

A. Causation: General Information

In some cases, causation is straightforward, while in other cases, it is more complex. An example of a straightforward situation would be the following: John was a passenger on a boat that smashed into a dock, rendering him a paraplegic. It is clear in this scenario that the driver of the boat caused John's paraplegia, leading to his damages.

Other cases are not so straightforward. Consider this situation: Jane's car was hit by a trucker who drove through a stop sign. Jane broke her ankle. Sounds pretty straightforward so far, right? But then you add a layer of complexity: Jane had a long history of pre-existing problems with the same ankle. She had an awful recovery from the injury she suffered in the car because of her pre-existing ankle problems. While an average person would have had a normal recovery, Jane will never walk again without a cane.

Should the at-fault trucker have to pay all of Jane's damages? He did not cause the initial ankle problems that contributed to her poor recovery from this car crash. The court, in this instance, would have to determine the extent to which Jane's current and future ankle problems, giving rise to her damages, were caused by this car crash. As you can imagine, these types of cases can be complex.

This leads us to what lawyers refer to as *thin skull* and *crumbling skull* cases.

B. Thin Skull and Crumbling Skull Cases

Thin skull and *crumbling skull* cases arise from situations in which an injured person had a pre-existing medical condition.

They are referred to in these terms because of an old case that was decided in England in the early 1900s.[14] In that case, a man who had a genetically thin skull suffered a head injury. His injuries were unexpectedly severe because of his (pre-existing) thin skull.

Over the years, case law has developed in such a way that an at-fault party has to "take their victim as they find them."[15] In other words, at-fault parties are responsible for the person's injuries or losses, despite the fact that these may be more extensive than those

---

14 *Dulieu v. White & Sons*, [1901] 2 KB 669.
15 *Athey v. Leonati*, [1996] 3 S.C.R. 458.

one might expect of an average person.

The thin skull rule applies across the board, to people who have pre-existing physical, psychological, or other medical conditions. As long as the person's pre-existing condition was stable, the at-fault party is responsible for their losses, even though they are more severe than normally expected. For example, if a person suffers from a stable pre-existing psychological or physical vulnerability such as depression or a broken bone, and then another person commits a wrongful act that injures them, the injured person is entitled to their full level of damages.

While personal injury lawyers will often argue that their client had stable pre-existing vulnerabilities rendering them thin skulled, the insurance defence lawyer will often respond with a crumbling skull argument. In other words, the defence will argue that the pre-existing condition was not stable. They will say, rather, that the condition was deteriorating and that the injured person is in no different position than they would have been if the wrongful act had not occurred. If the insurance defence lawyer is successful with their crumbling skull argument, then the at-fault party will only have to pay to the extent that their wrongful acts worsened the injured person's pre-existing condition.

The key to the distinction between the thin skull argument and the crumbling skull argument is whether the pre-existing condition was stable or not. If the pre-existing injury was stable, the injured person collects their full damages despite the unexpectedly bad outcome. On the flip side, if the defence proves that the pre-existing injury was not stable and really had no impact on their current condition, then the injured person does not collect the full extent of their damages.

Clear as mud, right? Legal causation is one of the more complex areas in personal injury law. The combination of medical and legal issues causes great difficulty for injured people, lawyers, judges, and juries.

4. The Standard of Proof

A. General Information

As you will recall, personal injury cases much be proven on a *balance of probabilities* – meaning something is more likely to have occurred than not. For example, in a case where it is alleged that a drunk driver hit and killed John, the family's lawyer must prove on a balance of probabilities (that it is more likely than not) that the driver was drunk and that he smashed into John and killed him.

B. Future Losses

Over the years, courts have recognized that proving future losses (for example, lost income, loss of housekeeping and home maintenance capacity), and anticipating higher future care costs, involves a degree of guesswork. In fact, the Supreme Court of Canada acknowledged that there is a degree of crystal ball gazing when projecting future losses.[16]

To accommodate this challenge, the standard of proof is lower for proving these future losses. The personal injury lawyer must prove that there is a "real and substantial *possibility*" that the injured person will suffer the loss. In other words, the lawyer must prove that

---

16   *Supra* note 9.

the losses are possible but does not need to prove they are probable.

This lower standard of proof is particularly important in cases involving severely injured children. In cases involving severely injured children, most of their losses will be future losses. Which career would they have enjoyed had they not been injured? What will their future care costs be by the time they reach age 50? While still challenging, the lower standard required to prove their losses makes it easier for an experienced personal injury lawyer at trial.

TEGGART'S BOTTOM LINE

Personal Injury Law 101 – What You Need to Know

- To be successful with a case, a lawyer must prove liability, causation, and damages
- Courts will assess whether someone other than the injured person is at fault. Lawyers refer to this as the **liability** issue in the case.
- Liability is usually proven by showing that someone fell below the standard of care expected of the average, reasonable person. This is also referred to as the **tort** of negligence.
- Courts may divide fault between different parties. This process is referred to as **apportionment of liability.**
- Courts may decide that the injured person was wholly or partly at fault for their own injuries. This is referred to as **contributory negligence.** Any percentage fault attributed to the injured person will reduce the amount of money they receive by the same percentage.
- **Damages** refers to the money paid to a person who was injured or suffered a loss because of another person's wrongful act (negligence).
- Common **heads of damages** include:
    » loss of past income and loss of future earning capacity,
    » past and future care costs,
    » loss of housekeeping and home maintenance capacity,
    » pain and suffering and loss of enjoyment of life,
    » out-of-pocket expenses,
    » claims by family members of people injured or killed, and
    » punitive damages.
- Personal injury lawyers must prove that the wrongful act caused their client's injuries.

- People with pre-existing stable injuries (**thin skull** cases) are entitled to full payment for their losses even though their condition is worse – and their losses potentially greater than would be expected if the average person suffered the same injury.
- At-fault parties in cases involving pre-existing unstable injuries are only responsible to the degree that the wrongful act worsened their condition.
- The personal injury lawyer must prove the injured person's case on **a balance of probabilities** and not **beyond a reasonable doubt.**
- Future losses only need to be proven using the standard of a **real and substantial possibility.**

CHAPTER EIGHT

Starting to a Lawsuit

The personal injury lawyer must draft a document called a Statement of Claim to start a lawsuit. In this chapter, we'll learn about what a Statement of Claim is and how a lawsuit is started.

1. The Statement of Claim

A Statement of Claim (also referred to by lawyers as a *pleading*) is the document that starts a lawsuit. Once drafted, it is filed at a local courthouse and then served on the parties that are being sued. You'll find I have included a sample Statement of Claim in Appendix B.

Generally speaking, the Statement of Claim defines the issues in the lawsuit. It identifies the parties involved, how much is being sued for, what happened, what the allegedly responsible party did wrong, and the damages (pots of money) the injured person is claiming.

What follows, is a breakdown of the typical sections contained in a Statement of Claim.

A. *The Parties: Who is Suing Whom?*

The first page of Statement of Claim identifies who the parties are. The injured people and any family members intending to sue are identified as plaintiffs in the Statement of Claim. They are the people who are suing. The responsible person (or entities, in the case of a corporation) are identified as defendants; these are the people or entities that are being sued.

When the injured person is a minor or does not have the cognitive capacity to make their own decisions, a *litigation guardian* must be named to represent them in the lawsuit. A litigation guardian basically stands in the shoes of the injured person and instructs the personal injury lawyer when required. Usually a family member of the minor or person lacking capacity is chosen as the litigation guardian.[17]

The remainder of the first and second pages of the Statement of Claim is a boiler plate form that is prescribed by our Rules of Civil Procedure (court rules).

B. *The Prayer for Relief: How Much Is Being Claimed?*

The first paragraph of the claim itself is referred to as the *prayer for relief*. This is just a lawyerly way of saying "this is what the plaintiff is asking for." It sets out how much money is being sought and anything else the plaintiff is asking for. It usually includes an amount for disbursements (the lawyer's out-of-pocket expenses for

---

17 Litigation guardians are required to submit an affidavit confirming who they are, along with some other facts. The personal injury lawyer prepares the affidavit and it is also filed with the court.

prosecuting the case) and another amount for costs, which is how lawyers refer to legal fees.

Here is a warning that I always give to my clients when I provide them a copy of the Statement of Claim. Just because you are suing for $10,000,000 (for example) in the Statement of Claim does not mean that your case is worth $10,000,000. Personal injury lawyers choose the amount to sue for based on a variety of reasons.

C. Who Are the Parties and Where Do They Reside?

The next section of the Statement of Claim details where the plaintiff and defendant reside (or conduct business, in the case of a corporate defendant). This section is important because it identified the parties involved and also may serve to inform the court that it has jurisdiction over the dispute.

D. What Happened?

The next section of the Statement of Claim details what happened to whom, when, and where. For example, if it is a boating case, this section will describe when the incident happened, where it happened, and the details of what happened.

E. Allegations of Negligence

The next section of the Statement of Claim will detail what the plaintiff says the defendant did wrong. These are called *allegations of negligence*.

What is important to understand about this section is that these are just allegations. In other words, they have not been proven. In fact, there may be no evidence whatsoever that these allegations are true. The lawyer includes them, however, because at this early stage in the case, they don't have all the evidence. By including these allegations in the Statement of Claim, the lawyer can ask questions about them at the *examinations for discovery* which you'll learn about in Chapter 9.

F. Injuries and Impairments

In this section of the Statement of Claim, the plaintiff's injuries and impairments are described. It's my practice to take the description of my client's injuries directly from the medical reports. This way, there are no mistakes.

In terms of impairments, lawyers scour the rehabilitation reports for all of the impairments the injured client is suffering from.

By the end of the case, a client may be suffering from some—but not all—of the injuries and impairments mentioned in the rehabilitation reports. This is perfectly fine from a legal perspective and is to be expected as part of the healing process. The point, however, is to include everything at the beginning because it is impossible to know which impairments will become permanent.

In fatal injury claims, this section will be short. It will simply describe the fact that the person died as a result of the injuries they suffered.

G. Claims for Damages

In the sections that follow, the different heads of damages that the plaintiff is seeking payment for are described (see Chapter 7 for a description of the types of damages that may be claimed). For example, in a typical personal injury case, the plaintiffs will be claiming damages for loss of earning capacity/income, the costs of past and future medical expenses, general damages for pain and suffering, loss of housekeeping and home maintenance ability, and damages for loss of care, guidance, and companionship under the *Family Law Act*.

H. Legislation and Place of Trial

There are certain laws the personal injury lawyer must cite because they will be relying on them in the case. These are included in the Statement of Claim so that a judge is aware of them at a later date.

Finally, the place of trial will be named. Usually the place of trial is chosen based on where the injured person resides, where the personal injury lawyer practices law, or where the incident that led to the lawsuit happened.

2. Jury Notice or Not?

Unless the case involves a government entity (for example the Province of Ontario), or the case is started under the Simplified Procedure rules or Small Claims Court rules (where damages claimed are less than $200,000), the plaintiff is entitled to have a jury decide the case.

Some plaintiff lawyers are comfortable having juries decide cases, while others would prefer that a judge alone decide the case if it were to go to trial.

The personal injury lawyer will draft and serve a *Jury Notice* if they want to have a jury decide the case.

Unlike juries in criminal cases, which have twelve members, a jury in a personal injury case is made up of six members of the community.

3. Will My Case Go to Trial If I Sue Someone?

While there are no guarantees, the reality is that most personal injury cases (over 90 percent, according to statistics) settle before trial. Does this mean that your case won't go to trial? No. But it does mean that there is a good chance that it will settle.

4. What Happens If I Change My Mind and Decide Not to Sue?

It may be possible to get out of a lawsuit you have started—depending on the circumstances. The best rule of thumb to follow is that it is easier to get out of a lawsuit earlier rather than later. If the lawsuit was started within six months of your wanting to get out of it, there is a good chance you will be able to do so. It can be more difficult if you wait a number of years after starting the lawsuit to decide that you want out. The reason is that by this time, the insurance company will have spent significant amounts of money on lawyer's fees to defend against your claim. It may be that they will want you to compensate them for this.

The best advice I can give is that if you want to get out of your lawsuit, talk to your personal injury lawyer about it as early in the process as you can.

5. What Happens After the Lawsuit Is Started?

After your lawsuit is started, the insurance company for the defendant will assign a lawyer to defend against your case. This lawyer is commonly referred to as the defence lawyer or the insurance defence lawyer.

The insurance defence lawyer will review your file and prepare a response to your Statement of Claim. They will file it with the court and serve it on your lawyer.

The insurance defence lawyer's response to your Statement of Claim is called a Statement of Defence. Basically, it is the flip side of the Statement of Claim. While you may never see the Statement of Defence, I can guarantee you that it will deny virtually everything that is claimed in your Statement of Claim. It will even go so far as to blame you for an incident that wasn't your fault.

I wouldn't get upset about this. What the defence is basically saying is, "Prove it!" Proving it will be up to your personal injury lawyer.

Like the plaintiff's lawyer, the insurance defence lawyer also has the right to file a Jury Notice. The case will be decided by a jury if either the plaintiff's lawyer or the insurance defence lawyer file a jury notice barring a court order otherwise.

TEGGART'S BOTTOM LINE

Starting a Lawsuit

- A personal injury lawyer starts a lawsuit by drafting and filing at a courthouse a document referred to as a **Statement of Claim.** This is then served on all of the parties to the lawsuit.
- The Statement of Claim defines the issues in the case and includes the following:
    - the names of the parties involved, including the plaintiff (or injured person) and the defendant (the person who committed the wrongful act);
    - the **Prayer for Relief** which states how much the plaintiff is suing for;
    - what happened, where it happened, and when it happened;
    - allegations of negligence (what the defendant did wrong);
    - a list of the plaintiff's injuries and impairments, or a statement that the person died as a result of their injuries;
    - the plaintiff's claims for damages (e.g., loss of earning capacity, future care costs, loss of home maintenance capacity, and pain and suffering); and
    - reference to the relevant laws and the place of the proposed trial.
- The personal injury lawyer will decide whether or not to ask that the case be tried with a jury. Juries are not allowed in certain cases involving government entities and cases started under the Simplified Rules where the damages claimed are less than $200,000.
- Just because someone starts a lawsuit does not mean that there will eventually be a trial. The vast majority of cases settle before a trial takes place.
- It is possible for an injured person to withdraw their lawsuit if

they change their mind. The later this happens, the more likely the defence will ask that a portion of their legal fees be paid.
- The defendant's insurance company will hire a lawyer. The insurance defence lawyer will prepare, file, and serve a response to the Statement of Claim. The responding document is called a Statement of Defence. In the Statement of Defence, the defendant will deny all of the allegations made by the plaintiff in the Statement of Claim.

CHAPTER NINE

Examinations for Discovery

After the lawsuit is started and the insurance company has defended the case, the next stage in the legal process is to arrange *examinations for discovery*. This is an important part of every serious personal injury case.

In this chapter, you'll learn what examinations for discovery involve, typical areas of questioning by insurance defence lawyers, and some tips that may help make this meeting most productive for you as you work towards a successful case.

1. What Are Examinations for Discovery?

Examinations for discovery are an out-of-court question-and-answer session conducted under oath. Both the plaintiff and defendant will be required to attend at different times to answer questions about the case. Your lawyer will have the chance to ask the defendant questions. At a separate time, the defence lawyer will have the chance to ask you questions—with your lawyer present. While entitled to do so, the defendant does not usually attend a plaintiff's examination for discovery session.

The insurance defence lawyer will know a lot about your case before your examination for discovery. This is because your lawyer is required to give the defence lawyer many documents beforehand in what is called an *Affidavit of Documents.*

An Affidavit of Documents contains records that are relevant to the case, including records from the police, the hospital, doctors, and rehabilitation professionals. It also may include OHIP records, employment files, and tax returns. Hopefully, the insurance defence lawyer will have reviewed these documents before the examinations for discovery and will know a lot about the case before the first question is asked. This process of producing documents is called *documentary discovery.*

Examinations for discovery are an important step in the lawsuit process. It allows both your lawyer and the insurance defence lawyer to understand your case better. In addition, the answers that you give can be used in the future by medical experts, accident reconstruction experts, and even at trial.

2. Where Do Examinations for Discovery Take Place?

The examinations for discovery are conducted in a court reporter's office. This is not a courtroom and there is no judge present. The court reporter's role is to record the questions the insurance defence lawyer asks and the answers that you give to these questions. These answers are then referred to as evidence. Ultimately, the court reporter may be called upon to create a transcript of your evidence.

3. What Do I Wear to My Examination for Discovery?

This is a very common question. Many folks believe that they have to wear formal clothes to the examinations for discovery. In fact, they do not. It's important that people feel comfortable in this unfamiliar situation. While there are no strict rules about dress, it's never a bad thing to make a good impression. Dressing neatly and not overly casually, is usually a wise idea.

4. Typical Areas of Questioning by the Defence Lawyer

While every case is different, defence lawyers typically ask questions about a number of different topics. At the risk of oversimplifying, the following is a list of the topics that the defence lawyer will ask you about (in no particular order):

- your life before your injury, including your employment and/or education;
- any physical or mental health problems you had before your injury;
- your lifestyle, including recreational pursuits you had before your injury;
- how your injury happened;
- the treatment you have received since your injury;
- what you are able or unable to do because of your injuries; and
- any further injuries you have suffered since the incident.

In the case of fatal injury claims, family members will be asked questions about their deceased family member's life, any pre-existing physical or psychological problems the deceased may have had, and the impact the death has had on them. While they may be asked about the incident that led to the death of their family member, it is understood that in many cases, family members may have only limited information.

Reading the above lists may lead you to believe the examination for discovery will be easy. In fact, this is not often the case. Part of the insurance defence lawyer's job is to ask you questions that will reveal answers that help their client's case. It's important to keep this in mind throughout the process and to speak with your lawyer about the best way to handle any difficult questions.

It is normal to feel anxious before your examination for discovery. My practice is to meet with clients in the week ahead and fully prepare them. This kind of meeting really helps to reduce anxiety, as I am able to let clients know what to expect. Fear of the unknown is something we all experience. Once people have a better picture of how the examination for discovery works, they tend to feel much less anxious and much less nervous about this part of the lawsuit process.

5. Preparation for Your Examination for Discovery

While the specific advice I provide my clients in advance of their examination for discovery varies from case to case, there is some general advice I give all my clients, regardless of the nature of their personal injury claims. This is divided into two simple categories of dos and don'ts:

DO	DON'T
• Tell the truth.	• Guess at the answer to a question. You can provide an estimate if you have a reasonable one but guessing will help no one.
• Say, "Yes" or "No" as opposed to "Mmhuh," because a transcript is being made. Unless you are clear, nobody will be able to understand your answer when reading this transcript later.	• Argue with the defence lawyer.
• Ask for clarification or advise that you don't understand a question if that is the case.	• Be sarcastic with the defence lawyer.
• Answer only the question that is asked.	• Answer questions that your lawyer objects to, even if you think the answer won't hurt your case
• Be polite.	• Object to questions yourself.
• Say, "I don't remember" if you don't remember the answer to a question. People are rarely able to recall the answer to every question.	• Ask your lawyer if you have to answer a question. Unless they object, you do need to answer the question.
• Take a break if you need one.	• Bring notes or diaries to the examination for discovery.

6. How Do Examinations for Discovery Work?

The short answer is that the insurance defence lawyer will ask you questions that are relevant to the different pots of money that form your case, as discussed in Chapter 7. But let's unpack that a bit to give you a better idea of how things work.

You will attend the court reporter's office on the day of the examination for discovery. Your lawyer will bring you into a boardroom where this meeting will be conducted. At one end of the boardroom table, you will see a court reporter, set up with a computer and ready to take down the questions asked, along with the responses. You will meet the insurance defence lawyer(s) and take a seat with your lawyer on one side of the table. The insurance defence lawyer(s) will sit on the other side of the table. The number of insurance defence lawyers on the other side of the table is a function of the number of parties you sued—these are the defendants in your lawsuit.

Before the examination for discovery starts, the court reporter will ask you whether you want to take an oath to tell the truth on the Bible, or if you would rather simply *affirm to tell the truth*. Either option is perfectly acceptable, so you can choose whichever feels most comfortable to you.

In the event that the case involves a minor or a person without legal capacity, then their litigation guardian will be the one answering the questions.

Your examination for discovery will start once you have taken the oath or affirmed to tell the truth. This is what lawyers refer to as being *on the record*.

Throughout your examination for discovery, you will find that the insurance defence lawyer will have discussions with your lawyer. They will probably ask your lawyer for a laundry list of documents relevant to your case that they don't yet have. Your lawyer will tell the defence lawyer whether or not they will agree to produce these. If your lawyer agrees to produce certain documents relevant to your case, these are called *undertakings*. If your lawyer doesn't want to give the defence lawyer the documents then these are referred to as *refusals*.

7. Do Examinations for Discovery Have Rules?

The examination for discovery has rules that govern how it works. The most important rule is that the insurance defence lawyer is only allowed to ask questions that are relevant to the claims you have made in your lawsuit.

So, who determines whether a question is relevant to your lawsuit? The answer is twofold. At the examination for discovery itself, your lawyer determines what is relevant and what is not relevant. If your lawyer believes that a question from the defence lawyer is not relevant, then your lawyer will object to the question and you won't have to answer it. If this happens, the defence lawyer can then present the question to a judge at a later date. At that point, the judge will make a decision, and either require you to re-attend to answer the question, or agree that you do not have to answer it.

It is your lawyer's job to ensure that the insurance defence lawyer sticks to questions that are relevant to your claims and follows the rules. When objecting to a question, my personal practice is to put my hand up in front of my client (as a visual cue to my client), tell them not to answer the question, and give the insurance defence lawyer the reason for my objection.

8. How Long Will My Examination for Discovery Last?

Every case is different, so it is hard to say how long your examination for discovery will last. Some defence lawyers, particularly younger lawyers, tend to take a long time with their questioning. More senior lawyers won't take as long. Your lawyer may be able to give you a sense of how long they expect the process to take. Suffice it to say that it will likely last a minimum of an hour and could potentially take all day—or even longer—in more complex cases.

Rest assured that if your examination for discovery turns out to be lengthy, you'll be given the opportunity for lunch and any other breaks you require throughout the day.

In smaller personal injury cases involving claims for damages of less than $200,000 (caught by the Simplified Procedure referenced at the beginning of the book) examinations for discovery are limited to three hours. Your personal injury lawyer will be aware of this time limitation.

TEGGART'S BOTTOM LINE

Examinations for Discovery

- **Examinations for discovery** are an out-of-court question-and-answer session.
- Your lawyer will meet with you in order to prepare you before your examination for discovery.
- Before the examination for discovery, your lawyer is required to produce many documents relevant to your case.
- During the examination for discovery, the insurance defence lawyer will ask you questions about your case, with your lawyer present.
- Your lawyer will object to any inappropriate questions. You do not have to answer questions your lawyer objects to unless a judge later orders you to do so.
- At a separate time, the defendant(s) will attend examinations for discovery and your lawyer will ask questions relevant to the fault issues in the case. You do not need to attend the examination for discovery of the defendant.
- The basic rule of examinations for discovery is that lawyers can ask questions that are relevant to issues in the lawsuit.
- You may feel anxious before your examination for discovery. This is entirely normal, and as you become more familiar with the process, your anxiety will most likely diminish.

CHAPTER TEN

Post-Examination for Discovery Events

There is a lot to do following examinations for discovery. Some of this will happen behind the scenes, so to speak, and you won't even know about it. You'll have a front-row seat to other aspects, though. In this chapter, you'll learn about what happens and the work performed that goes into building your case at this stage in the process.

1. Medical-Legal Examinations and Other Expert Reports

A. Your Medical-Legal Examinations

In most serious injury cases, the injured person's lawyer will refer them for medical assessments by a doctor (or doctors) of their choosing. Doctors do an examination, assess the injuries, and prepare reports to send to the lawyer. For example, if you suffered a brain injury and now have cognitive and psychological impairments, your lawyer might send you to a neuropsychologist and a neuropsychiatrist for assessments. They would each assess you and provide a report outlining their opinions concerning your diagnosis, prognosis, and future treatment options. In lawyer's language, these are referred to as *expert reports* or *medical-legal reports*.

Injured clients often misunderstand the purpose of medical-legal assessments, believing these are done in order to help them in the rehabilitation process. While you may have similar assessments done as part of your rehab process, these particular evaluations are done strictly for the legal case at hand.

Not every case will go to trial, but if yours does, the experts can be called as witnesses to give opinion evidence. Alternatively, the experts' reports can be filed as evidence. The opinions of these experts will serve, along with other medical documents, as the foundation for your claims for pain and suffering, loss of income, future care costs, and housekeeping and home maintenance costs. Without preparing reports that state their medical opinions formally, these experts would not be permitted to give evidence at a trial.

In addition to the opinions of doctors, it may be very important to retain a certified life care planner to review file materials, interview the treatment team, and give an opinion concerning what your future care needs will likely be, and provide an estimation of what it will likely cost to pay for necessary services. For example, in a case involving hip fractures, the life care planner would provide an opinion concerning the physiotherapy and any other kinds of non-OHIP-funded treatment the injured person might need following hip replacement surgery. They would also estimate the cost of these treatments.

B. Medical-Legal Examinations Required by the Defence

The defence is entitled to send you for medical-legal assessments of its own. They will choose their own doctors to assess you and provide reports setting out their opinions about your injuries and prognosis, the impact on your education or employment, and future treatment requirements.

Remember that the defence is working on the side of the insurance company; the opinions of the doctors they select are probably not going to help your case. Here is a list of some predictable points defence doctors might argue in their reports:

- Your injuries are not as serious as your experts say they are—or perhaps you suffered no real injuries at all.
- The defendant did not cause your injuries; in fact, they were caused by an unrelated event or medical condition (see chapter 7 concerning the crumbling skull argument).
- The prognosis for your injuries is good; you should expect a full recovery or at least, a better recovery than described by the experts your lawyer retained.
- Your injuries will have no impact on your education or employment possibilities, or at least, will have less of an impact than that described by the experts your lawyer retained.
- You won't need the treatment recommended by the experts your lawyer retained.

It will then be up to your lawyer to send the defence medical reports to your experts for any rebuttal opinion and corresponding report that may be required.

C. Other Expert Opinions

Along with experts who can provide opinions concerning injuries and prognoses, personal injury lawyers may, in certain cases, retain additional experts to address other issues.

As an example, forensic engineers can bring opinions on the liability (or fault) aspects of a case. In a car crash case, a personal injury lawyer might retain a forensic engineer to prepare an accident reconstruction report that will establish what happened and who is at fault.

Another expert whose opinion can be very valuable is a forensic accountant or economist. Their role is to provide an opinion concerning the value of your case. They take the report of the life care planner and calculate the present value of the recommended future care cost items over the rest of the injured person's lifetime.

It is important to note that the calculations in fatal injury cases are different. In these cases, the forensic accountant or economist will calculate the present value of the claims of the family members who would have benefitted from the income the deceased person would most likely have brought into the family. They may also calculate the value of any family member's loss of earnings and future care costs.

Finally, an expert specializing in vocational education is able to provide an opinion concerning the impact of injuries on a person's ability to return to work or to complete their schooling, as the case may be.

2. Fulfilling Undertakings and Motions

The injured person's lawyer will also be busy fulfilling all of those undertakings (or promises to request documents) that were given at examinations for discovery. This may be a lot of work in serious injury cases, and your lawyer's team will expend a great deal of time and energy completing this task.

At this stage in the process, and even sometimes before examinations for discovery, your lawyer or the defence lawyer may bring *motions*. A motion is where a lawyer appears before a judge (or someone referred to as a *Master* in some areas) and asks the judge to make an *order* in your case.

The most common motion that personal injury lawyers bring is for the production of records from a third party. This happens often in car crash cases. The personal injury lawyer will bring a motion for an order requiring that the police produce their complete file concerning the investigation of the crash. They may have already produced a portion of the investigation file; however, personal privacy laws may have prevented them from disclosing all of the documents, and a motion and a court order are necessary to allow them to produce their entire file.

3. Focus Groups

As part of their trial preparation, experienced personal injury lawyers may conduct a focus group if a jury (as opposed to a judge) will be deciding the case. In the context of a personal injury lawsuit, a focus group is a gathering of people from the community who offer their opinions about the injured person's case.

Focus groups have a variety of different formats depending on the lawyer and the particular case. On one side of the spectrum, some lawyers may conduct a formal mini-mock trial and ask the focus group participants to make decisions similar to those that the jury will make. On the other side of the spectrum, the lawyer may lead the focus group in a less formal, guided discussion about the important aspects of the injured person's case.

Regardless of the format of the focus group, the lawyer is looking for feedback that will help them in their presentation of the case to the jury. Likewise, they may be looking for clues that will help them choose the type of jurors they want to decide the case.

TEGGART'S BOTTOM LINE

Post-Examinations for Discovery Events

- In serious injury cases, a personal injury lawyer will probably send their injured clients to doctors who will assess them and prepare a medical-legal report setting out their opinions concerning the injuries and prognosis. These opinions will help support the foundation of the case.
- A lawyer will likely have a life care planner assess the injured person to determine future care needs and anticipated needs for housekeeping and home maintenance assistance. This professional's opinion will help support the foundation of claims in the case.
- A vocational or educational expert may be retained to provide an opinion concerning the injured person's ability to complete schooling or work in the future. This opinion will help support the foundation of claims for loss of earning capacity.
- The injured person's lawyer will hire a forensic accountant or economist to calculate the present value for claims for loss of earning capacity, future care costs, and loss of housekeeping and home maintenance capacity.
- In fatal injury cases, a forensic accountant or economist will calculate the present value of the income losses suffered by family members who will not benefit from the future income of a deceased loved one.
- The insurance defence lawyer is entitled to arrange defence medical examinations with doctor(s) of their choosing. The doctors will make assessments and prepare reports detailing their opinions concerning injuries and prognoses.
- The defence doctors will probably not support your case.

Furthermore, they may say any combination of the following, amongst other things:
- » Your injuries or prognosis are not as bad as other doctors say.
- » You will fully recover from your injuries.
- » Your injuries are unrelated to the incident for which you have sued, and the defendant is therefore not responsible.
- » You will not actually need the future care or support that the life care planner hired by your lawyer has suggested you will require.

- Your lawyer may ask your experts to provide a written response to the defence's medical opinions.
- Your lawyer may bring motions to the court asking a judge to make certain orders in your case. A typical motion a personal injury lawyer might bring is for the police to produce their entire investigation file.
- Your lawyer may arrange to conduct a focus group if a jury (as opposed to a judge) will be deciding your case. The focus group will help your lawyer in their future presentation of the case to the jury.

CHAPTER ELEVEN

Mediation

Over the last 20 years, mediation has become a popular way to bring together the parties to a lawsuit in an effort to try to settle the case. In fact, mediation is mandatory in some areas under our rules of court.

In this chapter you will learn what a mediation is, who attends, what their roles are, and how mediations work. You will also gain some practical advice about what to wear, and the appropriate mindset to have as you begin this process.

1. What Is a Mediation?

A mediation is an out-of-court meeting between the parties to a lawsuit, in which an effort is made to resolve the case by way of a settlement—without having to go to court. Mediation is often referred to as a form of *alternative dispute resolution*. This means that it is an alternative to going to court to resolve a dispute.

2. The Players: Who Attends a Mediation and What Are Their Roles?

A. *The Mediator*

A mediator is an impartial person who attempts to bring the parties together to resolve the lawsuit. While many mediators are lawyers who have practiced in the area of personal injury law or insurance law and know the field well, they also have special training in how to resolve disputes.

The role of the mediator is not like the role of a judge or arbitrator. The mediator does not tell the injured person how much to accept. Likewise, the mediator does not tell the insurance company representative(s) how much they should pay.

Their role, rather, is to review the issues, look for common ground and areas of dispute, and bring everyone together through negotiations at a settlement value that the injured person is willing to accept and the insurance company is willing to pay.

B. *The Injured Person, Their Lawyer, and Family Members*

Often, an injured person will bring along a friend or family member for support throughout a mediation. Sometimes the family members have Family Law Act claims and attend because of this. Whatever the reason for their presence, family members' attendance is perfectly acceptable.

The injured person must attend the mediation, and it is their job to instruct their personal injury lawyer on offers to make to the insurance company. In a fatal injury case, the family members will instruct their lawyer on offers to make throughout the process.

The personal injury lawyer also attends, and they have a number of jobs to do throughout the course of the mediation. First, they will conduct what is called an *opening* or *opening statement*. They will then provide advice on the strengths and weaknesses of the case, the offers to make to the insurance company, the offers the insurance company makes, and they will also advise the mediator of instructions the injured person has given.

It's important to point out that you are in charge at the mediation. That is, you decide on whether to accept your lawyer's advice and ultimately whether your case settles. Your lawyer's job is to provide you with advice, but they should not be making the ultimate decision as to whether or not your case settles.

If your case does settle at mediation, your lawyer will advise you about the legal releases that you will need to sign.

C. The Insurance Defence Lawyer and the Insurance Company Representative

The roles of the insurance defence lawyer and insurance company representative are basically the flip side of the roles you and your lawyer have. That is, the insurance defence lawyer will present an opening statement and conduct negotiations on behalf of the insurance company. The insurance company representative is the lawyer's client for the purposes of the mediation. Their job is to instruct their lawyer on offers to make.

It's important that you understand a few things about the insurance company and its representative who attends the mediation. First, you need to understand that the representative may come to a mediation with permission to pay only up to a certain amount of money. Lawyers often refer to this as their *authority*. This is kind of like a budget they have for your case. As bizarre as it sounds, the insurance company representative may not tell their own lawyer what their budget is for your case.

Second, depending on the seniority of the insurance company representative, they may have a boss—or even a committee of people they have met with before the mediation about the case. This committee has likely set the insurance company's authority or budget for the case.

Third, the insurance company representative may be able to call their boss during the mediation in order to request more authority (in other words, to increase the budget of what they can pay). In some instances, however, the boss or the committee responsible for making this decision is unavailable and the insurance representative will be limited to the authority they first brought to the mediation.

D. Others

From time to time, other non-parties (people who are not involved in the lawsuit) also attend the mediation of a case.

Representatives from an insurance company—whether they are handling accident benefits or no-fault insurance—may also attend mediations in car crash cases. This is usually done in an effort to *cash out* or settle the future value of your benefits claims. This process is kind of like getting a divorce from your no-fault insurance company. They agree to pay you money on account of your future benefits, and in exchange, you agree to accept the money and make no more claims to the insurance company.

At the time of the writing of this book, the Ontario Government is seriously considering getting rid of no-fault cash-outs. Many experienced lawyers feel this move could be disastrous for injured people and their families for a variety of reasons. Hopefully, expert input will help guide this decision.

Finally, from time to time in serious personal injury cases, a representative of a *structured settlement* company may attend a mediation. (Chapter 14 includes more information about structured settlements.) For now, it is helpful to know that the structured settlement representative really doesn't participate in the mediation. They attend in cases where it may be advantageous to the injured party to invest settlement funds in a structured settlement. Their role is to offer advice on structured settlements and explain the payments that could be generated if settlement funds were invested in one.

3. Before the Mediation, and Your Mindset Going into It

It's important to understand that the lawyers have done a lot of work in advance to prepare for the mediation.

A. Mediation Briefs

Both your lawyer and the insurance defence lawyer will have prepared a document called a *mediation brief*. This is a written document outlining each party's position. Mediation briefs are sent to the mediator and the opposing lawyer in advance of the mediation. They contain arguments and evidence that the lawyers anticipate introducing at trial. Briefs can be in the range of 20 or more pages and may incorporate sections of helpful evidence such as medical reports, witness statements, and reconstruction opinions. They also anticipate (and try to address) the arguments that the defence lawyer might make in their brief and mediation opening statement.

B. Meeting With Your Lawyer Before the Mediation

Typically, personal injury lawyers meet with their clients before the mediation. The purpose of this meeting is to review the process and what to expect at the mediation. Whether the lawyer provides their client with an appropriate settlement value or range at this meeting varies from lawyer to lawyer and case to case.

C. Expectations and Mindset

It's really important to come to the mediation with an appropriate mindset—one of cautious optimism. It's all right to think that there is a chance your case will settle at the mediation. People get themselves into trouble however, when they *expect* that their case will settle.

If you arrive at the mediation intent on settling, and then discover that the insurance company has vastly undervalued your case, it may just be difficult for you to switch gears and re-think whether settling is the best plan for you. It might just be tempting to settle—for too little—just to get the process over with.

I've done this work for over 22 years and have attended countless mediations. I know for certain that there is no predicting whether a case will settle at mediation; there are just too many variables. Because of this, I always counsel clients to bring a healthy sense of skepticism to the mediation. With this mindset, they are much less likely to settle for too little.

One last word of advice concerns spending money before you

receive it. During my career, I have been aware of several people who, during the course of their personal injury lawsuits, made big purchases before a mediation—in anticipation of their case settling. Imagine doing this, and then facing the possibility of a lower settlement than you expected. Knowing that you have a big bill to pay could make it very tough for you to make the best possible decision about settlement at your mediation. A wiser course of action is to wait until a settlement is formalized before spending any large sum of money.

4. How Does a Mediation Work?

A. *The Venue*

Most mediations happen at court reporters' offices[18], just like the examinations for discovery. You will arrive and your lawyer will escort you to the main mediation room. It will likely be a large boardroom with many chairs around a big table. Don't let this intimidate you; you are the most important person in the room!

Eventually the mediator, insurance defence lawyer(s) and their insurance company representative(s) will arrive. The mediator will sit at the end of the table. The insurance defence lawyer(s) and their clients will sit on the opposite side of the table from you.

---

18 As I write this book, some mediations are moving on-line in response to the Covid-19 outbreak. On-line or "virtual" mediations may be a trend we see in the future.

B. Preliminary Remarks by the Mediator

The mediator begins by introducing everyone around the table and offering some preliminary remarks. These remarks vary, but basically, mediators welcome everyone to the mediation and then speak directly to the injured person for a few minutes. They talk about the focus of the day being the resolution of your case. Some mediators warn injured people about misinterpreting any humour (or attempts at humour) during the mediation and assure them that all parties come to the table seriously and out of a desire to resolve the case.

C. Your Lawyer's Opening Statement

The mediator then turns things over to the injured person's lawyer to present their opening statement. The opening statement is meant to summarize the key issues and arguments in a party's case. Good lawyers will also address arguments that they anticipate the lawyer on the other side of the table will make in an effort to take the wind out of their sails.

The personal injury lawyer's opening can vary widely in both length and style. Some lawyers present their opening statement with a PowerPoint presentation (or something similar) that is projected onto a screen. Other lawyers simply tell the client's story.

One question that clients often ask me before a mediation is whether they have to say anything during the opening statements. The answer is no; the injured person is not obligated to speak. That said, some of the most powerful opening statements occur when both the lawyer and the injured person participate. This doesn't work well in every case, however; if your lawyer feels it would be helpful for you to say anything during the opening statements, they should plan this with you beforehand.

The length of the opening statement is really a function of the lawyer's style and the complexity of the case. It is reasonable to expect this part of the mediation to take between twenty and thirty minutes.

Be aware that it can be an emotional and very difficult experience to hear your lawyer speak about all of your losses. In this situation, where many people would feel anxious and stressed, you might just break down and cry. You should know that this happens all of the time and is entirely understandable.

D. *The Defence Lawyer's Opening Statement*

After the injured person's lawyer completes their opening statement, the mediator calls upon the insurance defence lawyer(s) to give their opening statements. The defence lawyer's opening will be shorter than that of the injured person's lawyer. This is just a function of how things work in a personal injury lawsuit. The injured person's lawyer has to build a case whereas the defence lawyer just has to poke holes in it.

The insurance defence lawyer's opening statement can also be difficult to listen to. This is because the defence lawyer is going to focus on all of the bad stuff in your case. And every case does have some bad stuff—things that detract from the value of the case.

You should not respond to the defence lawyer's opening statement even if you feel it is wrong or upsetting. You will have the rest of the day to respond through your lawyer if you wish. It is unwise to show that you are feeling distressed, so it's important to not respond verbally, and possibly emotionally, to what you hear.

E. Caucusing and Negotiations

After opening statements are complete, the mediator will invite everyone to *caucus*. Caucus is just a fancy word that means everyone goes to their own separate rooms. Most clients feel a tremendous sense of relief after opening statements are complete, because they no longer have sit in the same room with someone who is working against them. From this point onwards, they won't have to see the insurance defence lawyer or representative.

There is still a lot of hard work ahead, though. Usually, at this point the mediator will come to you and your lawyer and ask you to make an opening offer in your case. If they haven't done so already, your lawyer will give you advice on an appropriate first offer to make. They will ask you for your instructions on whether to make this specific offer. If you give them these instructions, they will advise the mediator of your offer. The mediator will then communicate your offer to the defence lawyer and insurance company representative. Then you wait.

Before mediations, I always recommend to clients that they bring something to do during the mediation. This is because there can be large gaps of time when you are waiting for a response from the insurance company to an offer you have made. A combination of boredom and anxiety often happens during this time. A book, a crossword puzzle, or your phone with a few favourite games may all help to pass the time and keep your anxiety at a minimum.

At some point, the mediator will return with a first counter-offer from the insurance company. A word of warning: they will not have accepted your first offer. In fact, it's more likely than not, that they will be making what you feel to be an insultingly low counter-offer. Some mediations abruptly end after the first insultingly low counter-offer because the plaintiff's lawyer realizes that the defence did not come prepared to settle the case.

If the negotiations continue after the first counter-offer, then the process moves forward. The offers will likely get better from here on. This back-and-forth of offers and counter-offers may continue for a long time.

Along with the counter-offers, the mediator will discuss arguments that the insurance company is making. For example, the insurance company may argue that you are significantly at fault for the incident that led to your injury. Or, they may argue that your lawyer's argument concerning loss of income is flawed because there is a chance you will work again. In short, you can expect that the insurance company will make every argument it can to try to limit the amount of money it has to pay you.

This can be unsettling, but it is par for the course. It happens in every case. Don't take it personally. The reality is that the insurance company is in business to make money. The more they pay you, the less money they make.

F. Settlement

The bottom line is that if, at the end of the day, you come to an agreement about what you are willing to accept, and what the insurance company is willing to pay, then your case settles.

If this agreement is achieved, my personal practice is to obtain a written direction from my client to settle their cases. The written direction confirms the amount of the settlement and my client's net recovery after legal fees are paid. It may also contain other conditions relevant to the settlement. My client will read and sign the direction. Once they do so, I advise the mediator of my instructions to settle the case.

In some cases, the insurance company will have a legal release for you to sign at the mediation. In other cases, you will have to wait a few weeks to receive and sign the legal release.

Once you sign the legal release, your case is legally settled. If it was signed at the mediation, the insurance company *requisitions* the money. This means that they ask the head office for the money.

Many people believe that the insurers just have the settlement funds easily accessible, but this is not the case. It can take up to a couple of months for the insurance company representative to receive the money from head office and get it to you.

5. What Happens If My Case Doesn't Settle at a Mediation?

In reality, mediators are unable to settle many personal injury cases. Every case is different, and the list of reasons mediations fail is endless. Sometimes, it can even happen that the reason a mediation fails is a factor that is out of everyone's control.

Many injured people and their families wonder what happens if their case does not settle at a mediation. Do you go straight to trial? Does this mean that the case will never settle?

The short answer is no to both of these questions. Just because a case does not settle at a mediation doesn't mean that it will not resolve at some point later in the process. In fact, based on the statistics, there is a high likelihood it will settle at some point.[19]

---

19 The statistics about settlement are not entirely clear, however, it is generally believed that over 90 percent of civil cases settle.

In some cases, there may be more than one mediation. A second mediation is another opportunity to resolve the case.

Depending on the area where your lawsuit was started, the next step following mediation will be to prepare for, and attend, a pre-trial conference before a judge. You'll learn about pre-trial conferences in the next chapter.

TEGGART'S BOTTOM LINE

Mediation

- A mediation is an out-of-court meeting between the parties to a lawsuit. An impartial mediator will attempt to bring the parties together to settle the lawsuit.
- Cautious optimism is a good attitude to bring to the mediation. People who are convinced that their case will settle are often disappointed. Even worse, they may end up settling their case for less than a fair amount.
- The lawyers will prepare lengthy mediation briefs in advance.
- The lawyers will present openings that summarize each of their arguments.
- Negotiations will begin after the openings are completed.
- You are in control of the offers to settle that you make at the mediation. Your lawyer will give you advice on the offers to make, but it is up to you whether or not to accept your lawyer's advice.
- Before any settlement, I prepare written directions for my client to read and sign. These give me the authority to settle their case. The written direction will confirm the amount of my legal fee and my client's net recovery (what they receive) after payment of legal fees. Once my client has signed the written direction, I advise the mediator of the settlement.
- If the case settles, the injured person (or the family in a fatal injury case), will be required to sign a legal release confirming the settlement.
- If the case settles, the money will take some time to arrive. As a general rule, it can take a month or more to receive the settlement funds.
- Many cases do not settle at mediation for a variety of reasons. This doesn't mean the case won't settle at some point in the future.

CHAPTER TWELVE

Pre-Trial Conferences

If your case didn't settle through informal negotiations, or at a mediation, then the next step in the process is to attend a *pre-trial conference*.

1. What Is a Pre-Trial Conference?

A pre-trial conference is a meeting between the lawyers and a judge. It is meant to narrow the issues of the case, deal with procedural matters, and discuss the merits of the case—even, potentially, including settlement.

A pre-trial conference happens after one of the parties to a lawsuit files a document called a *trial record*. By filing the trial record, the party is letting the court know that they are ready for the case to proceed to trial. The court will then arrange a date for the pre-trial conference.

The lawyers will prepare for this conference in a similar way to how they prepare for a mediation. The lawyers will prepare a brief and submit it to the court in advance of the conference. This brief will be a written summary of each party's arguments and positions.

The purpose of the pre-trial brief is to disclose each party's positions on the case. It will inform the presiding judge about the case and the positions that each party is taking. Likewise, it will inform the opposite party of the positions that will be taken at trial. It will contain arguments on the important issues in the case in an effort to persuade the judge and the opposite party of the strength of the case.

It is important to point out that the judge who presides over this conference will not be the same judge that presides over the trial if the case proceeds to trial. Our court rules prohibit the pre-trial conference judge from presiding at any future trial in the case.

2. How Does the Pre-Trial Conference Work?

All of the important players are required to attend the pre-trial conference. The injured person (or family members, in fatal injury cases) and their lawyer attend, along with the defence lawyer and a representative of the insurance company.

Upon arrival at the courthouse, there will be written *dockets* (labels or signs) displayed to point people in the right direction. That is, the dockets list what is happening in each courtroom throughout the day, including the names of the presiding judges. You find the dockets, look for the name of your case and then find the courtroom listed for your case. In larger courthouses (like those in Toronto or

Mississauga), it can be challenging to find the listed courtroom. It's a good idea to arrange an easy meeting place with your lawyer and have their cell phone number with you just in case.

While the docket will list a courtroom or a room number for your case, this does not mean that your pre-trial conference will happen in that location. It may happen there, but it also could take place in a judge's chambers (their office), the judges' library, or a courthouse boardroom.

When the time comes for the pre-trial conference to start, a court services officer will usually come and speak to all the lawyers to ensure everyone is present. Following this, they will bring the lawyers into the room where the conference will be held.

The judge will probably want to meet with the lawyers first. In fact, there are cases when the injured person and insurance company representative do not meet the pre-trial conference judge at all. Whether there is a meeting or not is a function of the case and the judge's particular preference.

What happens at the pre-trial conference varies from case to case and judge to judge. The judge will have read each party's brief. They may start by asking questions of the lawyers or they may start by inviting the lawyers to make *submissions*, or arguments about their cases. More often than not, a judge will provide their opinion on the issues in the case at the pre-trial conference.

In some cases, the judge will attempt to help the parties settle the case. They may meet with each lawyer alone to gain a better sense of whether settlement is possible. They may also meet with the lawyer and their client. Offers to settle may be exchanged throughout the process, and arguments may be made back and forth between the lawyers.

There will be limited time available for the pre-trial conference. Court dockets are usually full, and the judge only has so much time to participate before having to move on to the next case on the docket.

If the case does not settle, then the judge will deal with certain procedural issues with the lawyers. They will discuss the anticipated length of the trial, the number of witnesses involved, and whether particular issues can be dealt with ahead of time. Finally, plans will be made for a trial date to be booked.

If your case does not settle at a pre-trial conference, does this mean that you go to trial? Not necessarily. In some cases, judges conduct multiple pre-trial conferences. In other cases, the judge's opinion in the case causes the lawyers and clients to re-think their settlement positions. Many cases resolve following a pre-trial conference because of the opinions expressed by the judge.

TEGGART'S BOTTOM LINE

Pre-Trial Conferences

- A **pre-trial conference** is a meeting between the lawyers and the parties to a lawsuit to discuss the case. Amongst other issues, the judge will discuss the possibility of settling the case.
- The judge presiding over the pre-trial conference will not preside over any future trial. A different judge will preside over the trial if the parties are unable to resolve their dispute.
- The pre-trial conference judge will probably meet with the lawyers first.
- The judge may or may not wish to meet with the injured person (or family members in fatal injury cases).
- The judge will probably give their opinion about the case.
- Some cases settle at pre-trial conferences often because of the opinions expressed by the judge.
- If a case does not settle at the pre-trial conference, there is still a possibility that it will settle before trial.

CHAPTER THIRTEEN

Trial

While most cases settle without having to go to trial, it is important to have a general understanding of how trials work. In this chapter, you'll learn about the factors that influence the length of a trial, how lawyers pick a jury, and some other important details about trials in general.

1. How Long Does a Trial Last?

It is difficult to speculate on how long any particular trial will last, as there are a few factors that play a role in the process.

First, if cases are brought under Ontario's new Simplified Procedure rules (which apply when less than $200,000 is claimed), trials are limited to a maximum of five court days.

The second determining factor is the complexity of the case. Generally, cases involving complex issues of liability and damages will last longer than more simple cases, in which the issues are straightforward.

The third element that affects trial time is whether a jury is involved. Jury trials generally take longer to complete than cases in which a judge alone is making the final decision.

The fourth factor that may influence the length of a trial is the availability of both the judge and the courtroom. It is entirely possible that because of limitations on the availability of either the judge or the courtroom, the trial might not proceed on consecutive days. That is, there could be interruptions along the way, during which the court cannot sit. As an example, a trial could proceed for a week, and then break for a week or more, due to scheduling or other conflicts. This is not at all uncommon in busier courts like Toronto's and Brampton's.

On a final note, you should understand that your lawyer might ask you to be present for the whole duration of the trial or, they might only ask that you come to testify. This is a strategic decision the lawyer will make and varies from case to case and lawyer to lawyer.

2. Jury or No Jury?

A number of factors dictate whether a jury or a judge alone will decide a personal injury case. These factors include the following:
- whether a party to the lawsuit served a *Jury Notice* at the beginning of the case; if none was filed, a judge alone will decide the case;

- whether a government entity is involved; juries are not permitted in cases involving a government entity such as the province or a municipality;
- how much money the injured person claimed in the lawsuit; no jury is available in personal injury cases covered by the Simplified Procedure rules (which apply to claims less than $200,000).

3. Choosing the Jury

Choosing the jury in a personal injury case is a relatively straightforward process. First, the court provides the lawyers with a list of potential members for the jury. These people are chosen through the jury duty system in which Canadians participate. The list includes the name and occupation of each potential juror.

The court then arranges for a panel of potential jurors to attend the courthouse for the jury selection process. The group—often large enough to fill the room—files into the courtroom where a judge is presiding.

The judge tells the panel of potential jurors a little about the case, in an effort to identify and exclude those who might have a conflict of interest. The judge may read out the names of the parties involved and the basics of what the case concerns, and then invite potential jurors who may know a party to the lawsuit or have some knowledge of what happened to raise their hands. So, for example, if the plaintiff's best friend or treating medical professional happened to be in the jury pool, the judge would exclude them from being picked as a juror for the case.

The judge will also deal with potential jurors who do not want to serve for one reason or another. The reality is that some people see jury duty as an inconvenience and resent the idea of having to serve. Some potential jurors may legitimately state that they have scheduled medical procedures, trips, or family or business obligations that conflict with serving on the jury. The judge will make rulings regarding the selection of jurors and will move ahead with the process.

Unlike criminal trials, in which twelve jurors decide a case, only six jurors decide personal injury cases. Also, unlike criminal cases, these six jurors do not have to come to a unanimous decision; it is sufficient if only five of the six jurors agree on a verdict.

Once the group of potential jurors are in the courtroom, the judge calls the names of six of them. They are invited to sit in the jury box at the front of the courtroom.

Each of the lawyers present then has four *"peremptory challenges."* In other words, each lawyer has the right to exclude a maximum of four jurors for any reason. If there is more than one defendant in the case, their lawyers receive a total of four challenges altogether, and they must decide how many each will get.

Once each lawyer has used all four of their challenges, or is content with the selected jurors, the jury is set.

You may be wondering what prompts a lawyer to use a challenge for a particular juror when they only have the potential juror's name and occupation. Each lawyer considers the facts of the specific case and makes decisions accordingly. If they have conducted a focus group in the case, then this may have helped them identify the type of jurors they want to decide the case. The bottom line, however, is that the lawyers are just guessing about people. The lawyers have no idea whether a particular juror holds certain biases or opinions that may come to bear in the case. The lawyers involved may have views on the type of juror they want, but assessing whether or not potential jurors fit the profile they are hoping to see is really just speculation.

4. Pre-Trial Motions and Preliminary Issues

Before a case starts, the lawyers will speak to the Judge about preliminary issues and motions. They will likely discuss scheduling issues, such as the length of the trial and days that the judge may be unavailable. They may also discuss scheduling conflicts that particular witnesses have.

The lawyers may have motions in which they ask the judge to make an order about a certain issue. Typical pre-trial motions in a personal injury case are as follows:

- A motion to refer to certain evidence in a lawyer's opening statement. Often a lawyer will want to refer to a particular piece of evidence or aid in their opening statement. For example, the injured person's lawyer may want to refer to photographs taken of the injured person in hospital, photographs of any damage to vehicles in a car crash case, or other important anticipated evidence. After hearing arguments from both sides, the judge will make a ruling on these issues.
- A motion to exclude witnesses from the courtroom. In this sort of motion, a lawyer would ask the judge to order that people who will be called as witnesses in a case not be able to sit in the body of the court until they are called on to testify.

- A motion to call more than three experts in the case. Under Ontario's court rules, the parties are only allowed to call evidence from three experts. In a serious personal injury case, however, the injured person's lawyer may want to call more than three expert witnesses such as doctors, engineers, and forensic economists or accountants. On the flip side, the defence will want to limit the number of experts who are permitted to testify for the injured person in the case. The lawyers will make arguments to the judge on this issue and the judge will then make a decision on the number of experts that can be called.

5. Opening Addresses

At the beginning of the case, each lawyer has the opportunity to give an opening address, which is a summary of the case from their own perspective. In particular, the lawyer will tell the judge and/or jury what they expect the evidence will be in the case.

Unlike what we see on television, there is a rule against arguing the case in an opening statement—lawyers are required to stick to describing what the evidence will include.

The lawyer for the injured person will present an opening address first. Each case is different, and every lawyer is different too; however, it can be expected that this opening address will last 45 minutes to an hour. In more complex cases the opening statement on behalf of the injured person may last longer.

Defence lawyers are not required to give an opening address at the beginning of a case. In fact, they may sometimes choose to delay their opening address until later in the trial for strategic reasons.

6. Simplified Rules Cases

In addition to not having juries and having trial time limited to a five-day maximum, cases started under the Simplified Procedures rules (where damages claimed are less than $200,000) differ in other ways from regular trials. For example, in Simplified Procedure trials, the plaintiff's case is presented by affidavit (a sworn written statement) instead of in person. The insurance defence lawyer then has the right to cross-examine the witnesses on their affidavits. Using Simplified Procedure rules is intended to shorten trials in which more modest amounts are being claimed. While they may be somewhat shorter, these trials still follow a similar arc to the longer, more serious personal injury cases in which damages claimed exceed $200,000.

The information that follows applies to these more serious cases.

7. The Plaintiff's Case

After the lawyers complete their opening addresses, the judge will call upon the injured person's lawyer to present their case. They begin by calling witnesses to testify. The testimony of the witnesses, and any relevant documents that are filed (like hospital records, for example) become evidence in the case. At the conclusion of the trial, the judge or jury will be called upon to make a decision based on this evidence.

In a typical case, the lawyer for the injured person will call many witnesses to testify. Witnesses can be divided into categories, including lay witnesses, expert witnesses, and treating medical witnesses.

A. *The Witnesses*

(i) Lay Witnesses

Lay witnesses are witnesses who have no special training relevant to the case. They are called upon to speak about their observations. These people might be friends, family members, colleagues, or even employers. Many will testify concerning their observations of the injured person before and after their injury, and their testimony is meant to show the impact of the injuries on the person's abilities and life in general. Lay witnesses may also testify concerning their observations of the incident that led to the person's injuries. For example, someone who observed a car crash might be called to testify about how the incident happened.

It is important to point out that lay witnesses are not allowed to give their opinion in a case. As an example, a lay witness could not give an opinion concerning the injured person's ability to work in the future, their medical diagnoses, or the type of care they might require.

(ii) Expert Witnesses

The injured person's lawyer will also call expert witnesses to provide their opinions in a case. These people fall into two general categories of expertise: damages and liability.

Depending on their specific area of expertise, damages experts may testify concerning the person's injuries, impairments, prognosis, future care needs, home maintenance needs, and income losses. For example, an orthopaedic surgeon who prepared a medical-legal report in the case might testify that a person suffered a fracture that extended into the ankle joint, and that they will most likely develop post-traumatic arthritis in their ankle—requiring surgery and treatment in the future. A vocational expert may testify that the person will likely have a shortened career as an iron worker because of their knee injury. A forensic accountant may testify and provide a calculation of how much money the injured person is likely to lose because of their shortened career as an iron worker.

Liability experts testify about the fault aspects of a case. For example, a forensic engineer who prepared an accident reconstruction report may testify about how a car crash happened, the speeds involved, and which lanes the vehicles were in when it occurred. A biomechanical engineer may testify about the mechanics of a crash and whether seatbelt usage might have made a difference.

(iii) Treating Medical Experts

Treating medical doctors might testify in a case even if they did not prepare a medical-legal report. The judge will decide whether they will be able to testify concerning the medical diagnosis and prognosis they provided to the injured person.

B. *Direct Examinations and Cross-Examinations*

The type of questions a lawyer can ask a witness depends on the lawyer's role. When an injured person's lawyer is presenting their case to the jury, they are only allowed to ask open-ended questions. These are the "who, what, when, why, and how" sorts of questions. They are not allowed to ask questions that suggest an answer to the witness. This latter type of question is called a *leading question* and is only allowed when asking questions of an opposite party's witness during cross-examination.

Here's a simple example to show the difference between an open-ended question and a leading question:

> Open-ended question (used in direct examination):
> *"What speed were you driving on Yonge Street in the 500m before the crash?"*

> Leading Question (used in cross-examination):
> *"You were driving your car 80 km/h on Yonge Street in the 500m before the crash?"*

C. How the Questioning Works

The injured person's lawyer will call a witness and the witness will take an oath or affirm to tell the truth. The injured person's lawyer will then start the direct examination of their witness. The injured person's lawyer can only ask witnesses open-ended questions when presenting their case to the jury. The point of the direct examination is to have the witness testify and provide evidence concerning particular issues that are helpful to the injured person's case.

Once their direct examination is complete, the defence lawyer is called upon to begin any cross-examination they intend to conduct. Sometimes, they may choose not to cross-examine the witness. Usually, though, they will take advantage of the opportunity and cross-examine the witness by asking leading questions. Generally, the point of cross-examination is to attack the injured person's case.

Following the cross-examination by the defence lawyer, the

injured person's lawyer is permitted to ask the witness questions to clarify any new evidence that came up during the cross-examination. This is called *re-examination*. As in the direct examination, the injured person's lawyer can only ask open-ended questions.

D. Completion of the Plaintiff's Case

Once the injured person's lawyer has finished calling all of the witnesses in their case, they advise the judge and/or jury that their case is complete.

It is then up to the insurance defence lawyer to begin calling witnesses for the defence.

8. The Case for the Defendant/Insurance Company

The insurance defence lawyer will call far fewer witnesses than the injured person's lawyer. Typically, they will call any lay witnesses they think will help the case, along with all of the experts that the insurance company paid to provide reports. They may also call a private investigator to testify concerning surveillance of the injured person, and to provide any video or photographs they took while following them.

The defence lawyer must follow the same rules noted above, asking only open-ended questions during direct examination of their witnesses.

After each of the defence witnesses has testified, the injured person's lawyer has the opportunity to cross-examine them, using leading questions if they wish.

9. Mid-Trial Conferences

In some cases, the judge presiding at a trial may arrange for another judge to conduct a *mid-trial conference*—a conference in which another judge will meet with the lawyers in cases where it may be helpful to get another educated opinion. While mid-trial conferences may vary, typically their purpose is to try to bring the parties together to settle the case. The second judge involved will call upon each lawyer to provide their views on how the case is going, and will make efforts to help settle the case.

Usually the injured person and insurance company representative do not participate in a mid-trial conference. If, however, the judge wants to impress their views directly upon them they may do so in the presence of their lawyers.

10. Reply Evidence

At the conclusion of the case for the defence, the judge will ask the plaintiff's lawyer whether they intend to call any *reply evidence*. This is evidence called to provide a rebuttal for any evidence given by the witnesses the insurance defence lawyer has called.

The plaintiff's lawyer is somewhat limited in the witnesses they may call in reply. Specifically, any witness called in reply must be presenting evidence that contradicts or qualifies facts or issues raised by defence witnesses. Otherwise, the judge will probably not allow the evidence of the witness to be called. Reply evidence is not overly common but is called from time to time in personal injury cases.

11. Closing Statements

After the defence closes its case, the lawyers present their closing statements.

Unlike opening addresses where the lawyers aren't allowed to argue the case, the lawyers are allowed to argue their case during closing statements. They review the evidence helpful to the positions they are taking, and the relevant law, and then make suggestions to the jury on how to answer the questions that will be posed to them, if the case is being tried with a jury.

Jury questions deal with the issues of fault and the losses suffered by the injured person. Some examples of the questions that might be put to the jury include:

Q. Have the plaintiffs satisfied you on a balance of probabilities that there was negligence on the part of the defendant, Joe Smith?

Q. If the answer to question #1 was "Yes," please state the particulars of the defendant's negligence.

Q. At what amount, if any, do you assess the damages suffered by the plaintiff for the following heads of damages:
- pain and suffering from the date of the crash and in the future?
- the plaintiff's loss of income from the date of the crash until today?
- the plaintiff's future loss of earning capacity from this date forward?
- the plaintiff's future care costs? (This head of damages may be broken down into numerous sub-headings

including medical and rehabilitation expenses, attendant care expenses, and expenses related to different potential scenarios that might arise.)

12. Charge to the Jury

In jury cases, the judge will *charge* the jury. In a judge's charge to the jury, they will review the evidence, the issues in the case, the positions or arguments each side is making, the law relating to the different issues in the case, the standard of proof, and suggestions as to how to consider the evidence—including how to assess the credibility of witnesses. Finally, the judge will review the questions that are posed to the jury.

A jury charge is meant to assist the jury in making a decision about the verdict in a case. In cases without a jury, the case is considered to be complete after the lawyers have finished their closing statements.

13. Jury Deliberations and Verdict

In a case with no jury, the judge will usually adjourn the case after the closing statements are complete. The judge will then take time to write a decision in the case. The judge's decision will address their findings on each of the issues in the case including which, if any, damages the injured person is entitled to.

In jury cases, the jury will retire to deliberate (make a decision) on each of the jury questions in the case. Once a minimum of five of the six jurors reaches agreement on each of the answers to the jury questions[20], they return to court. The jury foreperson will read the answers to the jury questions in open court, and their involvement is complete.

Usually, at this point a lawyer will then bring a motion to the judge for judgment in accordance with the answers to the jury questions.

Later, the lawyers will attend before the trial judge to discuss the amounts that will be awarded for costs and disbursements to the successful party.

---

20 The same five jurors don't have to agree on each of the jury questions.

TEGGART'S BOTTOM LINE

Trial

- It is difficult to speculate as to how long a trial will last. More complex cases take longer and trials with a jury take longer. Scheduling conflicts can often break up the trial over a lengthy period of time.
- Simplified Rules cases (when less than $200,000 is claimed by the injured person) may last a maximum of 5 days. They follow a different procedure than more serious cases. Evidence is given by affidavit. Lawyers may cross-examine the authors of affidavits.
- Jury trials are available in some personal injury cases. They are not available however in Simplified Procedure cases, or where a government entity (for example, a municipality) is being sued.
- In jury trials, the lawyers pick the jury from a panel of people called for jury duty. The personal injury lawyer can challenge up to four potential jurors and ask that they not sit on the jury. The insurance defence lawyer(s) can also challenge four potential jurors.
- The personal injury lawyer presents the case for the plaintiff first. This is done by witnesses giving evidence under oath. Typical witnesses in personal injury cases are lay witnesses (friends, family, and people who may have seen the injury happen), expert witnesses (doctors, accountants, and engineers) and treating medical witnesses.
- The insurance defence lawyer(s) will have the right to cross-examine the witnesses called by the personal injury lawyer to testify.
- After the personal injury lawyer has completed the case for the injured person (i.e., called all of the witnesses), the insurance defence lawyer has the right to call witnesses.

- The personal injury lawyer has the right to cross-examine the defence witnesses.
- After all of the evidence is presented, the judge (if there is no jury) or the jury (if there is one) will render a verdict. The verdict will address who was at fault and any money awarded to the injured person.

CHAPTER FOURTEEN

Life After a Lawsuit

In this chapter you'll learn about some common experiences following a settlement or verdict. You'll learn about how the government treats the proceeds from a lawsuit from a tax perspective. Finally, I will leave you with some solid advice about speaking to people about your case and the related topic of making a will and power of attorney.

1. Is It Really Over? The Right to Appeal

If a case is settled before the end of a trial then there will be no appeal in the case.

If a case goes to trial and a verdict is rendered, however, it is possible that either the injured person or the at-fault person will appeal the case.

An appeal is where a party asks the Ontario Court of Appeal to decide if a mistake was made (usually by the trial judge) during the trial.

An appeal to the Ontario Court of Appeal can delay the resolution of a case until the Court hears the arguments on appeal and makes a decision. After an unsuccessful appeal to the Ontario Court of Appeal, in a small number of cases, a party might appeal the decision to the Supreme Court of Canada.

Appeals are fairly frequent following personal injury trials. Sometimes an appeal is brought and used as leverage to try to negotiate a settlement in the case that is more favourable than the judgment was to a particular party. Other times, appeals are brought to ask for an outright reversal of the lower court's decision.

Appeals are beyond the scope of this book. Suffice to say, however, that if a case goes to verdict, there is a possibility that the decision will be appealed. This can delay the resolution of the case.

2. How Does It Feel to Have the Case Behind You?

Unlike what many people believe, very few people are happy at the end of their case, regardless of the outcome. I talk to my clients about how they feel and there is no question that resolving a personal injury case is a profoundly emotional experience. It is a reminder of the traumatic, life-changing event that led the person to see me in the first place. At the same time, there is a sense that the future is uncertain and a bit scary. Many of them know that their medical condition will deteriorate over time. They know that the physical and emotional scars they carry will be with them for life regardless of the money they may have received for their losses.

While everyone is different, over the years I have found that injured people and their families experience relief, above all else, once their cases resolve.

The relief they feel often comes from the fact that they know their lives will no longer be under the insurance company's microscope. They know they can now go about their lives without private investigators following them around or trolling any social media accounts they may have kept active. In short, they feel they have regained some measure of their personal privacy.

Relief also comes from the knowledge that they will have money to pay for their future healthcare expenses, replace the income they lost, and afford the necessities of life.

The harsh reality, however, is that some injured people will not have enough money to meet their future needs. In some cases, there is just not enough money in the insurance system to pay for their losses. In other cases, the injured person was mostly at fault (contributorily negligent) for their injuries and they will only receive a fraction of the funds they will likely require.

In one way or another, injured people know that the money the insurance company paid for their losses will never replace the health they enjoyed before their injury. And unfortunately, money is the only possible form of compensation for them. While I know firsthand from my seriously injured former clients that money makes a huge difference in their lives, it is certain that their lives will never be the same.

3. Taxation of Money from Settlement or Verdict

It is important to understand that a personal injury lawsuit can settle at any time. Some less complex cases can settle following negotiations with an insurance adjuster—before a lawsuit is even started. On the other end of the spectrum, some cases settle during the course of the trial or even after a verdict and before an appeal is heard.

Many people ask whether the money they receive from a personal injury lawsuit is taxable. While I am not an accountant, I've been doing this work long enough to tell you that money received in a personal injury lawsuit is not taxable.[21] That said, any interest earned on this money later is taxable.

While the money from a lawsuit is not taxable, it may affect the benefits you are entitled to from government programs such as CPP Disability and the Ontario Disability Support Program (ODSP). This is something that your lawyer may discuss with you, depending on the severity of your injuries.

4. Structured Settlements, Investments, and Finances

Many seriously injured people—and in particular seriously injured children and adults lacking legal capacity—choose to invest their settlement funds in a structured settlement. In fact, in a serious injury case involving a child or adult lacking capacity, a judge will be asked to approve the settlement and will likely insist that a significant portion of the settlement funds be invested in a structured settlement.

A structured settlement is a tax-free investment that is only

---

21 Please note that money received from non-personal injury lawsuits may be taxable. You should consult your lawyer and tax professional if you are dealing with money received from a non-personal injury lawsuit.

available to people who are resolving personal injury claims. A portion of the settlement funds is invested with one of a small number of life insurance companies in Canada. The life insurance company will then provide the injured person tax-free payments for a period of time and possibly for the rest of their lives.

Structured settlements are available in any successful personal injury case; experienced personal injury lawyers will discuss this tool with their clients and may then involve a structured settlement broker. The injured person will meet with them (at no cost), and will learn details about how structured settlements work, and the many benefits options available to them.

Whether you invest in a structured settlement or not, it is a good idea to consult with a financial expert at the end of your case. They can provide a strategy to make the most of your money. Your personal injury lawyer may be able to recommend someone who can assist you.

5. Don't Discuss the Settlement or Verdict Amount

I always recommend that my clients not discuss their settlement or verdict amount with anyone. Over and over I have seen so-called friends coming out of the woodwork after a lawsuit is resolved, and attempting to take advantage of the injured person, who may be in a somewhat vulnerable position at this time.

Aside from the professionals that you may need to discuss financial issues with (investment experts, structured settlement experts, accountants, etc.), you would be wise not to discuss your finances with others.

6. Have a Will and Power of Attorney Prepared or Reviewed

Following the resolution of a personal injury case, I always recommend that my clients see a wills and estates lawyer. It is important to have a will and power of attorney, and to ensure that these are up to date following the resolution of their case.

It is important to note that dying without a will likely means that family and beneficiaries will be faced with a government and administrative nightmare. In addition, the people you want your assets to go to upon your death may not even receive them.

The same thing goes for powers of attorney. Should you lose the capacity to make decisions for yourself at some point in the future, it is important to have designated a person (or people) to make important decisions for you.

I know this is the last thing most people want to think about, but it truly is an important issue.

TEGGART'S BOTTOM LINE

Life After a Lawsuit

- Money for a personal injury settlement or verdict is not taxable. If the money is invested, however, the interest earned on it is taxable—unless the investments were in a structured settlement.
- A structured settlement may be an appropriate investment, particularly in larger personal injury cases. Experienced personal injury lawyers will arrange for their clients to meet with a structured settlement broker to explain the options available to them.
- Consult a financial expert who can work with you on a strategy to make the most of your money.
- Don't discuss the settlement or verdict. You'd be surprised by the number of so-called friends who become financial vultures after a person's case is resolved.
- See a wills and estates lawyer to have a will and power of attorney prepared. If you already have a will and power of attorney, make an appointment with your lawyer to review them.

Glossary of Personal Injury Law Terms

Affidavit of Documents. A sworn statement to which a collection of documents relevant to the lawsuit is attached.

caucus. A closed meeting between a lawyer and their client that occurs after opening statements at a mediation.

Contingency Fee Retainer Agreement. A contract between a lawyer and their client that describes, among other things, a percentage legal fee that the lawyer will charge based on the client's financial recovery in a lawsuit.

contributory negligence. When the actions or inactions of a person are considered to have been a factor in their own injuries or death. In the context of personal injury law an example might be the injured person's not having worn a seatbelt or helmet.

costs. The amount paid to a successful party in a lawsuit to reimburse them for a portion of their legal fees.

cross-examination. The questioning of a witness who has already testified—usually for the opposite party. This questioning is used to attack the witness' testimony, and is often done using leading questions that suggest a desired answer. See contrast with *direct examination* below.

damages. The money paid to a person who was injured or suffered a loss because of another person's wrongful act

defendant. A person or company that is being sued.

direct examination. The questioning of a witness by the party that called the witness to testify. Direct examination is usually done using open-ended questions (including who, what, when, where, and why). Direct examination is also referred to as *examination in chief*.

disbursements. Expenses paid by a lawyer to pursue a case on behalf of their client. In the context of personal injury cases, disbursements include fees for hospital, employment, or income tax records, OHIP records, police records, clinical notes and records of healthcare providers, and other expert reports.

documentary discovery. The sharing of documents that each party to a lawsuit is required to provide to the opposite party. Documentary discovery is part of the *examinations for discovery* process.

examinations for discovery. The oral testimony of parties to a lawsuit given in advance of a trial. People giving testimony are asked to take an oath or affirmation to tell the truth before starting the examinations for discovery.

examination-in-chief. The questioning of a witness by the party that called the witness to testify. Direct examination is usually done using open-ended questions (including who, what, when, where, and why). Examination-in-chief is also referred to as *direct examination*.

insurance defence lawyer. A lawyer hired and paid by an insurance company to defend a lawsuit started against a person or company that it insures.

liability. Legal responsibility or fault for a person's acts or omissions.

liability insurance. Insurance that protects an insured person from claims made against them. Under a liability insurance policy, the insurance company is typically responsible for paying for successful claims against the person or company it insures, as well as legal costs and disbursements.

mediation. An out-of-court meeting between the parties to a dispute in which a mediator attempts to resolve the dispute.

mediation brief. A written document prepared by lawyers outlining their client's case. Mediation briefs are drafted and served on all lawyers and the mediator before the mediation.

motion. A legal process in which a party to a lawsuit asks a court to decide an issue in the case.

negligence. A failure to take reasonable care to avoid the injury of, or loss by, another person or group of people. A person will be found negligent (or at fault) if their actions or omissions fall below the standard of care of a reasonable person.

plaintiff. A person who brings a lawsuit against another. In the context of a case for personal injury damages, the plaintiff can be the injured person, or the family members of a person injured or killed.

pleading. A written legal statement detailing a party's claims in a lawsuit.

pre-trial conference. A meeting between a judge, lawyers, and clients in advance of a trial. The purpose of the pre-trial conference is to narrow the issues, address scheduling issues, and even the potential settlement of claims before going to trial.

re-examination. The second round of questions sometimes asked of a witness following their cross-examination. For example, a plaintiff's lawyer may ask a witness questions. This would be followed by cross-examination by the insurance defence lawyer. Then, the plaintiff's lawyer may re-examine the witness on issues arising from the cross-examination.

reply evidence. Evidence called by the plaintiff's lawyer after the conclusion of the case for the defence that is meant as a rebuttal or to clarify evidence given by a defence witness.

Statement of Claim. A legal document describing the claims of a plaintiff, including the amount for money claimed and the basis upon which the claims are being made. A lawsuit is started by filing a Statement of Claim in a court office and serving it on the defendant(s) in the case.

Statement of Defence. A legal document describing the claims of a defendant in a lawsuit. The Statement of Defence is filed in a court office and served on the plaintiff(s) in the case.

structured settlement. A legal settlement paid out via an investment called an annuity. In Ontario, structured settlements are only available in personal injury cases. Of note, these annuity payments are not taxable.

tort. A wrongful act leading to civil liability. In the personal injury context, the most common tort is negligence. Many lawyers refer to a person's claims for personal injury damages as their *tort case*.

tortfeasor. A person or company that commits a wrongful act against another.

undertakings. A promise to do a certain thing—usually given by a lawyer at examinations for discovery. In the personal injury law context, undertakings are often made to request hospital, rehabilitation, and other records from treating healthcare providers.

APPENDIX A

Accident Benefits Summary Chart

Type of Benefit	Minor Injury Guideline	Non-Catastrophic Impairment	Catastrophic Impairment
Medical & Rehabilitation	$3500 maximum	$65,000 maximum combined with attendant care Available for five years, or until age 28 for minors	$1,000,000 maximum combined with attendant care benefit Available for life or until benefit is exhausted
Attendant Care	Not available	$65,000 maximum combined with medical/rehabilitation Maximum of $3,000/month Available for life or until age 28 for minors	$1,000,000 maximum combined with medical and rehabilitation benefit Maximum of $6,000/month Available for life or until benefit is exhausted
Income Replacement		If a person is unable to return to work, they can receive 70% of gross income up to a maximum of $400/week Benefit is not payable for the first seven days after an accident. Benefit becomes more difficult to qualify for after two years post-accident	
Non-Earner		If a person is unable to carry on a normal life, benefit is payable at $185/week Payable for a maximum of two years but not for the first four weeks post-accident	
Caregiver		Not Available	If unable to engage in caregiving activities this benefit is payable at $250/week for the first person in need of care plus $50/wk for all other persons in need of care Maximum of two years unless the caregiver is still unable to live a normal life two years post-accident
Housekeeping and Home Maintenance		Not Available	Maximum of $100/week Available for life
Lost Educational Expenses		Up to $15,000 payable to those enrolled in school who are unable to continue with their program due to their accident	
Damage to Clothing		Reimbursement for damage to clothing, and/or medical or dental devices	
Visitor Expenses		Available to immediate family members for two years after the accident	Available to immediate family members for life
Transportation		Only available for distances longer than 50 km travelled	Available for all distances
Case-Manager		Not available	Available
Death Benefits		In cases of fatality, benefit of $25,000 to spouse, $10,000 to former spouse, and $10,000 to each dependant	
Funeral Benefits		Up to $6,000 towards funeral expenses	

APPENDIX B

Example Statement of Claim

Court File No.:

ONTARIO
SUPERIOR COURT OF JUSTICE

BETWEEN:

JOHN SMITH

Plaintiff

- and -

TIMOTHY JONES and SARAH WILLIAMS

Defendants

STATEMENT OF CLAIM

TO THE DEFENDANTS:

A LEGAL PROCEEDING HAS BEEN COMMENCED AGAINST YOU by the Plaintiffs. The claim made against you is set out in the following pages.

IF YOU WISH TO DEFEND THIS PROCEEDING, you or an Ontario lawyer acting for you must prepare a Statement of Defence in Form 18A prescribed by the Rules of Civil Procedure, serve it on the Plaintiff's lawyer, or where the Plaintiff does not have a lawyer, serve it on the Plaintiff, and file it, with proof of service, in this Court office, **WITHIN TWENTY DAYS** after this Statement of Claim is served on you, if you are served in Ontario.

If you are served in another province or territory of Canada or in the United States of America, the period for serving and filing your Statement of Defence is forty days. If you are served outside Canada and the United States of America, the period is sixty days.

Instead of serving and filing a Statement of Defence, you may serve and file a Notice of Intent to Defend in Form 18B prescribed by the Rules of Civil Procedures. This will entitle you to ten more days within which to serve and file your Statement of Defence.

IF YOU FAIL TO DEFEND THIS PROCEEDING, JUDGMENT MAY BE GIVEN AGAINST YOU IN YOUR ABSENCE AND WITHOUT FURTHER NOTICE TO YOU. If you wish to defend this proceeding but are unable to pay legal fees, legal aid may be available to you by contacting a local Legal Aid office.

TAKE NOTICE THIS ACTION WILL AUTOMATICALLY BE DISMISSED if it has not been set down for trial or terminated by any means within five years after the action was commenced unless otherwise ordered by the court.

Date:

(Local Registrar)
Issued by..............................

Address of Court Office:
75 Mulcaster Street
Barrie, ON L4M 3P4

TO: **TIMOTHY JONES**
123 MAPLE STREET
SOUTHLAND, ON A1A 2B2

AND TO: **SARAH WILLIAMS**
123 MAPLE STREET
SOUTHLAND, ON A1A 2B2

CLAIM

1. The Plaintiff, John Smith, claims:
   (a) Damages in the amount of $20,000,000;
   (b) Pre-judgment interest pursuant to the provisions of section 128 of the *Courts of Justice Act*, R.S.O. 1990, c. C.43;
   (c) Post-judgment interest pursuant to the provisions of section 129 of the *Courts of Justice Act*, R.S.O. 1990, c. C.43;
   (d) Costs of this action on a substantial indemnity basis; and
   (e) Such further and other relief as this Honourable Court may deem just.

THE PARTIES

2. The Plaintiff, John Smith ("John"), resides in the City of Barrie, in the Province of Ontario. He was the operator of a motor vehicle ("the Plaintiff motor vehicle").
3. The Defendant, Timothy Jones, resides in the Town of Southland, in the Province of Ontario. He was the operator of a motor vehicle ("the Defendant motor vehicle").
4. The Defendant, Sarah Williams, resides in the Town of Southland, in the Province of Ontario. She was the owner of the Defendant motor vehicle.

THE COLLISION

5. On November 1, 2019, the Plaintiff motor vehicle was travelling westbound on Main Street approaching Simcoe Drive in the City of Barrie, in the Province of Ontario.
6. At the same time, the Defendant motor vehicle was travelling eastbound on Main Street approaching Simcoe Drive.

7. Suddenly and without warning, the Defendant motor vehicle turned north in front of the Plaintiff motor vehicle intending to proceed onto Simcoe Drive.
8. The vehicles came to a violent collision causing the plaintiff motor vehicle to be propelled into the air and flip several times before smashing into the pavement ("the Collision).

NEGLIGENCE

9. The collision was caused solely as a result of the negligence of the Defendant, Timothy Jones, for whose negligence the Defendant, Sarah Williams, is responsible at law.
10. The Defendant was negligent in that:
    (a) He made an improper left turn;
    (b) He made an unexpected left turn and collided with the Plaintiff;
    (c) He failed to keep a proper lookout;
    (d) He failed to yield to the Plaintiff motor vehicle;
    (e) He failed to activate his horn to notify others of his presence;
    (f) He operated the Defendant motor vehicle without due care and attention;
    (g) He failed to apply his brakes properly, or in the alternative, the brakes of the Defendant motor vehicle were defective;
    (h) He moved quickly from a place of safety into a place of danger without taking reasonable precautions;
    (i) He allowed himself to become distracted;
    (j) He failed to have proper control of the Defendant motor vehicle;
    (k) He operated the Defendant motor vehicle in such a manner as to cause a violent collision with the Plaintiff motor vehicle;

(l) He was travelling at an excessive rate of speed;

(m) He was operating the Defendant motor vehicle while talking or texting on a mobile telephone or was operating any other electronic device;

(n) He was suffering from a medical condition that he knew or ought to have known would have prevented him from safely operating the Defendant motor vehicle;

(o) He was operating the Defendant motor vehicle when his ability to do so was impaired by the use of medication;

(p) He was operating the Defendant motor vehicle when his ability to do so was impaired by drugs or alcohol, or by both;

(q) He was incompetent to operate the Defendant motor vehicle with normal care and attention because his faculties of observation, perception, judgment and self-control were impaired due to physical and mental condition at the time of the collision;

(r) He operated the Defendant motor vehicle when his ability to do so was impaired by fatigue;

(s) He was an incompetent driver lacking in reasonable skill and ought not to have attempted to operate the Defendant motor vehicle on the occasion in question;

(t) He was operating a motor vehicle which he knew or ought to have known was not in fit and proper condition for safe operation on the road;

(u) He was operating a vehicle that was unsafe to other users of the road;

(v) He failed to take reasonable care to avoid a collision which he knew or ought to have known was likely to occur; and

(w) He failed to observe the rules of the road as required by the *Highway Traffic Act*, R.S.O. 1990, c. H.8.

INJURIES AND IMPAIRMENTS

11. As a result of the collision, John suffered injuries causing permanent, serious impairment of important physical, mental, and psychological functions.
12. John's injuries include, but are not limited to the following:
    (a) Acute spinal cord injury (C7 Asia A) with quadriplegia;
    (b) A severe fracture dislocation of his C6-7 vertebrae requiring a posterior spinal instrumented fusion, open reduction and fixation of the C6 vertebrae, open reduction and fixation of the C7 vertebrae, and C6-7 anterior cervical discectomy;
    (c) C7 vertebral body fracture;
    (d) Paralysis of the right vocal cord;
    (e) Fracture of the lower left second premolar; and
    (f) Bruising and a general wearing, tearing, and straining of the muscles, nerves and connective tissue throughout his body.
13. As a result of his injuries, John currently suffers from numerous impairments. His impairments include but are not limited to:
    (a) A loss of ability to walk;
    (b) Difficulty utilizing a wheelchair;
    (c) Severe bradycardia triggering several bradycardic arrests which made a transvenous pacemaker insertion necessary;
    (d) Absence of sensation in his lower extremities;
    (e) Absence of motor function in his lower extremities;
    (f) Decreased sensation in his upper extremities;

(g) Decreased strength in his upper extremities;
(h) Decreased sensation in his trunk;
(i) Difficulty eating;
(j) A loss of ability to transfer independently;
(k) A complete lack of control over bowel and bladder functions which requires the use of a catheter;
(l) Anxiety;
(m) Depression;
(n) Dysphagia;
(o) Autonomic dysreflexia;
(p) Fainting; and
(q) Dizziness.

DAMAGES

14. As a result of his injuries and impairments, John has undergone various and extensive forms of medical treatment and rehabilitation, which will continue for the rest of his life. He will require 24-hour attendant care for the rest of his life. John claims damages for the cost of his past and future medical, rehabilitation, attendant care, and other healthcare expenses.

15. John is permanently unemployable. He claims damages for his past loss of income and future loss of earning capacity.

16. As a result of his injuries and impairments, John will continue to suffer pain, emotional distress, and cognitive impairments that will permanently impair his enjoyment of life. He claims damages for his pain and suffering and loss of enjoyment of life.

17. As a result of his injuries and impairments, John is unable to perform housekeeping and home maintenance chores. He will

require paid assistance in the future to complete such chores. He claims damages for his loss of housekeeping and home maintenance capacity.

18. As a result of his injuries and impairments, John has incurred and will continue to incur out-of-pocket expenses. He claims damages for his out-of-pocket expenses.

LEGISLATION

19. The Plaintiff pleads and relies on the provisions of:
    (a) the *Highway Traffic Act*, R.S.O. 1990, c. H.8;
    (b) the *Courts of Justice Act*, R.S.O. 1990, c. C.43;
    (c) the *Negligence Act*, R.S.O. 1990, c. N.1; and
    (d) the *Insurance Act*, R.S.O. 1990, c. 1.8.

THE TRIAL

20. The Plaintiff proposes that this action be tried at the City of Barrie, in the Province of Ontario.

Date:

WILLIAM J. TEGGART
PERSONAL INJURY LAW
Professional Corporation
85 Bayfield Street, Suite 200
Barrie, ON L4M 3A7

William J. Teggart (41060D)
Tel: (705) 503-3385
Fax: (705) 503-5585

Lawyer for the Plaintiff

Made in the USA
Monee, IL
14 February 2021